CHAIN MAIL

** ADDICTED TO YOU **

WRITTEN BY HIROSHI ISHIZAKI

POP FICTION

STORY	Hiroshi Ishizaki
TRANSLATION	Richard Kim
ENGLISH ADAPTATION	Rachel Manija Brown
LAYOUT	Erika Terriquez
COVER DESIGN	Al-Insan Lashley
JUNIOR EDITOR	Kara Stambach
SENIOR EDITOR	Nicole Monastirsky
DIGITAL IMAGING MANAGER	Chris Buford
PRODUCTION MANAGER	Elisabeth Brizzi
MANAGING EDITOR	Vy Nguyen
ART DIRECTOR	Anne Marie Horne
EDITOR-IN-CHIEF	Rob Tokar
VP OF PRODUCTION	Ron Klamert
PUBLISHER	Mike Kiley
PRESIDENT AND C.O.O.	John Parker
C.E.O. & CHIEF CREATIVE OFFICER	Stuart Levy

First published in Japan in 2003 by Kodansha Ltd., Tokyo.
English publication rights arranged through Kodansha Ltd.
English text copyright © 2007 TOKYOPOP Inc.

Library of Congress Cataloging-in-Publication Data

Ishizaki, Hiroshi, 1958-
  [Chen meru. English]
  Chain mail : addicted to you / Hiroshi Ishizaki ;
[translation, Richard S. Kim ; English adaptation, Rachel
Manija Brown].
      p. cm.
  "First published in Japan in 2003 by Kodansha Ltd.,
Tokyo"--T.p.
verso.
  Summary: The boundaries between reality and fantasy
become blurred when four disillusioned Tokyo teenagers,
who have never met, collaborate to write an online fic-
tional story--a psychological thriller told from
four points of view.
  ISBN 978-1-59816-581-4
  [1. Interpersonal relations--Fiction. 2. Storytelling--Fiction.
3. Internet--Fiction. 4. Stalking--Fiction. 5. Mental illness--
Fiction. 6. Tokyo (Japan)--Fiction. 7. Japan--Fiction.]
I. Kim, Richard S. II.
Brown, Rachel Manija. III. Title.
PZ7.I82Ch 2007
[Fic]--dc22   2006031717

First TOKYOPOP printing: January 2007
    10 9 8 7 6 5 4 3 2 1
        Printed in the USA

PROLOGUE

"In this world, there is only one thing to be afraid of—when everyone's point of view is the right one."

JEAN RENOIR
<u>RULES OF THE GAME</u>

I stood in front of the mailbox and cried. Snow fell around me, frosting my hair and shoes, slowly blotting out the words of the test results I held in my hands. Out of over twenty-five thousand test-takers, I had placed first in Japanese, Mathematics, Science, Basic Studies, and General Studies. I had finally made it.

But it was too late. My mother was gone, and she wasn't coming back. If I had only studied harder, if I had only gotten these results a month earlier, maybe it would have made a difference.

Melting snow slid down my back. I shivered, remembering the sound of flesh striking flesh . . .

It had been a chilly night in November, before the snow had begun to fall. I lay on the floor of my room with my ear pressed to the door, listening to my parents rehash the results of that month's mock exam. My father's harsh voice was so loud that I could have heard him even if I'd been lying on my bed on the other side of the room. "Fifth place, huh?! Last month she was in third. This is your fault! You've been letting her slack off!"

I heard his fist slam into her soft body. Mama's tiny voice cried out, then I heard her gasp strained apologies. I flinched.

Every time the cram school* sent in my report card, my father got violent. I could imagine what was happening in the living room, as vividly as if I was really there: Mama backed up against the wall, covering her face with her arms. My father, punching her over and over. Her arms turning red and beginning to swell. Her hair falling to the ground after he'd ripped it off her scalp.

I wished I could save her. But I was afraid. I imagined standing in front of him, shouting, "Don't hit my mama!" Then he'd just turn his rage on me instead—I was terrified of his huge fists. All I could do was lie on the floor and be afraid for Mama.

The sound of my own heartbeats throbbed in syncopated rhythm to the blows his fists struck, and my breathing coincided with Mama's soft sobbing.

"*I* was always first in my class!" shouted my father. "Always number one! So if she isn't, it has to be *your* fault. It's because you're not disciplining her!" I could hear him hitting her at the end of each sentence like his punches were exclamation points. "Or else it's your bad genes coming out!"

I got off the floor, went to my desk, and opened a textbook. I put on earphones and turned on some music to drown out the other noises. I studied. If I could make first place, my father would have no excuse to beat Mama.

I studied during lunchtimes and late into the night. I stopped going out with my friends so I'd have more time to study. They weren't my real friends anyway—how could they be, since we were competitors? Anyone who got better grades than me became my enemy and the enemy of my mama. So I stopped talking to the other girls. It wasn't particularly difficult or painful, as long as I kept my goal in my mind: whatever it took, to save my mama.

But I had failed.

No, my father didn't kill her. Mama didn't die.

One day I came home and all that was left of her was a note pinned to my door:

---

* Schools in Japan that prepare students for university entrance examinations by way of an accelerated curriculum.

I wish I could have taken you with me, but I won't be able to afford to give you all the opportunities you deserve. I want you to get into a good junior high school, and then a good high school, and then a good college. But I can't pay for any of that. It breaks my heart to leave you, but I think that in the end, you'll be happier this way. I hope you'll understand.

There was no forwarding address.

If only I had made first place earlier, maybe I could have gotten a scholarship, and then Mama would have taken me with her. But now it was too late.

I had my prize, but no one to share it with.

I tore up the results of my latest mock entrance exam and flung them as far from me as I could. But the wind caught the bits and pieces of worthless paper, and blew them back into my face. They scattered around me and were swallowed by the gray slush on the ground.

The snow kept falling. I stood there, frozen in front of the mailbox, empty-handed and alone.

I.

"Bad air! Bad air! When something misbegotten comes near me, I must smell the entrails of a misbegotten soul!"

NIETZSCHE
<u>ON THE GENEALOGY OF MORALS</u>

FRIDAY, OCTOBER 3, 8:20 AM.

THE INTERSECTION IN FRONT OF THE ICHIGAYA TRAIN STATION.

Sawako walked through the ticket gate. Rain fell lightly, but the air was as hot and heavy as it had been in September, back when the second school term had started. Gray clouds hung low and oppressive overhead. As she waited at the intersection for the signal to change, the businessman beside her took out a handkerchief from his suit pocket and wiped the sweat from his thick neck. The white cloth quickly turned transparent.

Sawako edged away.

"Morning!" came a cheerful voice.

She turned around. The speaker was a girl in a black sailor suit. Sawako had no idea who she was or why a stranger had bothered to greet her . . .

"Hi, Miko!" Another girl came running up to meet the first one. "This rain sucks."

"Totally sucks," agreed Miko. "Hey, did you see 'Music Masters' last night? I thought the blond guy was so hot, didn't you?"

"*So* hot," echoed her friend.

Sawako quickly opened her umbrella. She didn't like the stifling humidity, but she did enjoy the rain because she could hide behind her umbrella. If she held it low, no one could see her face. And if no one could see her face, then no one knew who she was, and no one could drag her into idle conversations like the one the girls beside her were having.

What was the point of any of that? Maybe people liked to babble because the sound of their own voices (and other people's replies) were proof that they existed. Sawako wished they'd just look in the mirror instead.

The light turned green. Sawako hurried toward Yasukuni Street, leaving the other girls and their interminable discussion behind her. How many times had those girls had that exact same conversation? They probably kept talking right up until class started, and then they e-mailed each other on cell phones that they held under their desks. Sawako bet they went to the bathroom together, ate lunch together, walked home together, and then called and e-mailed each other from their rooms.

What is wrong with people? Why can't they stand to be by themselves? Is it so scary to be alone?

She walked up a hill and into the ritzy neighborhood of Nibancho. Elegant houses lined both sides of the street. Tall fences hid beautiful gardens, but she could see the tops of ginkgo and maple trees above the latticed wood, some with their leaves starting to turn scarlet or autumn gold. She could even hear the rain splashing into ornamental ponds. It was hard to stay angry here in this oasis of calm hidden in the center of the city. She stopped to peek through the tiny square gaps of a fence.

"Good day to you!"

Sawako spun around. It was the two girls from the Ichigaya intersection. They giggled in chorus, like a pair of clones, and shot her identical mocking smiles.

Sawako wasn't sure if she'd be teased more if she replied or kept silent. "Um . . ."

Both girls giggled again. "What's 'um' mean?" asked one of them—Sawako couldn't remember which one was Miko and which one was Miko's friend. "Is that Sawako-ese for 'good day to you'?"

"Six months in junior high and she still hasn't learned how to talk," said the other girl. She walked up and cuffed Sawako across the ear. "Speak, Nietzsche! Speak!"

Sawako jumped back and banged up against the fence.

The girls laughed shrilly. "Bad dog!" said one.

"No bone for you!" said the other.

Then, still giggling, the girls darted off toward the school. Sawako stayed where she was, leaning against the fence. She felt as if someone was strangling her. It was hard to breathe. She could hear her own heart pounding.

Other girls passed by, but though some gave her curious or taunting glances, none of them stopped to torment her further . . . or to offer her any help.

Sawako reached into her pocket and pulled out her cell phone. It was silver and shaped like a clamshell. She flipped it open and concentrated on the screen. At once, her panic began to ease.

She walked toward Kioi Academy, clutching her phone tightly. As she got closer to school, she started to hear voices:

"Hello!"

"Good day to you!"

"Great to see you!"

Sawako scowled. She scowled even harder when she remembered that she'd have to turn off her cell phone.

Kioi Academy was a famous private school for girls, an integrated junior/senior high school* that had an outstanding reputation for getting its students into excellent colleges. Its entrance examination was notoriously difficult and it expected a great deal of discipline from its students, but its motto was "freedom." It did not require

---

* In Japan, junior high covers USA grades 6-9; high school covers USA grades 10-12.

school uniforms, nor did it have a dress code or list of unacceptable hairstyles. But even the supposedly free-thinking Kioi Academy did not allow its students to use cell phones on campus, not even for emergencies.

Sawako moved her thumb toward the off button, but as she did so an envelope icon caught her eye. She didn't surf the Internet very much and rarely gave out her e-mail address, so she didn't get much spam. Her friends from elementary school knew her address, but she wasn't good at replying to messages, so her inbox usually stayed empty. There was one girl she'd made more of an effort to keep in touch with, but Sawako hadn't heard from her since before their last summer vacation.

She clicked on the message.

    Subject: Sawako, would you like to create a fictional
    world?

The message sounded like it could be from the girl who used to e-mail her, but that girl hadn't contacted her for almost a year. Sawako wondered if she ought to just delete it.

"Good day to you!"

Irritated, Sawako turned around. The girl who had addressed her was a third-year junior high school student and a member of the student council. She wore the unofficial "uniform" of the student council—expensive, top-of-the-line clothes. Her outfit resembled a regular sailor suit, but was beautifully tailored and sported a designer label.

"Don't forget to turn off your cell phone." The girl smiled, but Sawako was sure she was thinking something like, *I can't believe I, a junior and a member of the exalted student council, have to lower myself to lay down the law to a thirteen-year-old.*

"It's off." Sawako closed it with a snap and shoved it into her pocket. Ducking away from the student councilmember, Sawako hurried through the Kioi gates.

"Good day to you!" called the girl after her. It was sickening, actually.

If Sawako heard that insipid phrase one more time, she was going to throw up. Despite the "freedom" that Kioi Academy was so proud of, its sheep-like students had invented a ritual greeting that they chanted at every opportunity. No one knew who had started it, but somehow "Good day to you!" had become *the* phrase that everyone used to prove to each other—over and over and over again—that they belonged to the best school in the country. They chanted the phrase with identical smiles on their identical faces, rejoicing in their supposed superiority. In reality, it was simply mindless obedience to peer pressure.

Kioi Academy had been designed by a famous foreign architect before WWII, and unlike most of Tokyo, it had survived the American air raids. The surrounding buildings were made of wood or concrete, but the Academy was constructed almost entirely from massive chunks of gray stone. The ruthlessly symmetrical design, which eliminated all curves in favor of straight lines and right angles, was supposed to evoke a sense of security, but it made Sawako feel as if she was in an enormous jail cell.

She dashed down the oppressive corridors and ducked into a bathroom. If she got to class early, she'd just have to sit at her desk and listen to her classmates' stupid chatter.

Yuki Kanai stood inside the ladies' room, brushing her long hair and watching her reflection in the mirror. Sawako had never spoken to Yuki, but she'd heard that Yuki was a wild girl who practically lived in the nightclubs of trendy Shibuya.

Yuki gave Sawako a sharp glance as she came in, but didn't say anything. Instead, she adjusted the wide cloth belt on her fashionable pastel trench coat. Half the girls in Tokyo had one. The acceptable colors were white, khaki, pale blue, and pink. Yuki's was pink.

As Sawako headed for the farthest stall, Yuki spoke. "You're a freshman, aren't you?"

Sawako just nodded as Yuki applied a coat of mascara. The older girl gazed straight forward, meeting the eyes of Sawako's reflection. "Slaving away at your e-mail job?"

Sawako watched her own eyes widen in the mirror.

Yuki laughed. The red gloss on her lips shone in the florescent light. "You know, your online dating job. That's what you do, right? You get paid by a dating service to send dumb guys fake e-mails?"

Sawako finally realized what Yuki was talking about. There were a bunch of online dating sites that people could join if they paid a subscription fee. But they all had far more male subscribers than female ones, and so the men soon got discouraged and cancelled their subscription. A number of the sites paid women to pose as female subscribers and e-mail the men. They didn't have to meet them, only flirt with them online to keep them hooked and paying their dues. Sawako had heard that a lot of high school and junior high girls were doing it, but she'd never done it, nor did she have any desire to try it.

"Oh, n-no," she stuttered.

"Well, what are you doing, then? Every morning you come in here and write, write, write on that cute little shell phone. Are you writing to your boyfriend?"

Sawako blinked in confusion. She didn't have a boyfriend, and no one to write e-mails to. Yuki must have mixed her up with someone else.

"It's okay," said Yuki. "I won't tell anyone."

"It's not like that . . ." Sawako began.

"Or, if you *are* doing that online dating thing, I could tell you some better ways to make money."

"I'm just checking my e-mail," Sawako said firmly.

"All right. But if you ever want to earn a little extra cash, let me know. I know what people say about me, but I'm actually a very caring person." Yuki grinned and her teeth shone white against her wet, red lips.

Sawako's hands shook with a sudden jolt of fear. She nodded meekly, then stepped into a stall. The door slammed behind her, sending a long echo around the bathroom walls. She hung her umbrella and shoulder bag on the hook, then took her cell phone out of her pocket.

OCTOBER 3, 1:03 AM
SUBJECT: SAWAKO, WOULD YOU LIKE TO CREATE A FICTIONAL WORLD?

Hi. My name is Yukari. In case you can't tell from my name, I'm a girl. I'm a freshman at a private junior high school in Tokyo.

I'm sick of a lot of things. Aren't you? Like parents who keep nagging you to study, or the teachers who just act like glorified babysitters. But the people who piss me off the most are my so-called friends.

Last summer, this girl kept e-mailing me, but she never wrote anything interesting—it was always just, "What's up?" or "I'm bored. Are you bored too?" We were in the same class, but we'd never hung out together, so I didn't e-mail her back.

But when school started up again, everyone snubbed me. It turned out that the girl had e-mailed our entire class to tell them that I'd ignored her the whole summer, and that it would serve me right if everyone ignored me back. In case you're wondering how I found out (since no one would actually speak to me), another girl e-mailed me and told me everything.

I guess there was a lot of that going on, because I kept getting e-mails from girls who wouldn't talk to me in school, but felt free to write to me to complain about the girl who'd started the whole thing:

"FYI, she flunked her entrance exams, but they let her in anyway because her father's in the government."

"Heads up! Let me tell you the latest . . ."

Guess what? I'm not interested! If those girls are too chicken to talk to me in school, I couldn't care less what they wanted to tell me when it was safe for them.

I never responded to any of those e-mails either. So I'd never have to read another one, I changed my e-mail address. ^o^ And then everyone really did start ignoring me, in and out of school. It was such a relief! ^_^

I wonder if you understand how I feel. It's not that I don't want to have friends. I don't even hate e-mail. But I'm tired of messages that don't say anything, and people who won't stand up for what they believe in. If you're going to write anything at all, shouldn't you write something that's meaningful and fun?

That's when I had an idea. Let's all write a story together. It'll be a work of fiction, not a story about our real lives. But it'll seem so real that if anyone who didn't know what it was read it, it would terrify them.

Here's how it will work: I've come up with the plot of the story, and the four characters who'll be in it. You decide who you want to play. Then you pretend you're that character, and start writing from their point of view. You can write from your computer or your cell phone, then upload your piece of the story to our website.

Once your piece is up, another player will add to the story from the point of view of their character. I don't know what they'll write, or how the story will turn out. This isn't like school—there's no set rules and no predictable routines.

Sounds pretty cool, huh?!

If you feel the same way, go to the website and sign up. There's no fee to play. I just want this to be fun. But if you think you're a bad writer, please don't waste all of our time. In that case, Sawako, if you know someone who's got a little talent and a lot of imagination, please forward this message to them.

But only send it to someone you trust, someone who will hold up their end of the story. Real life is full of stupid people, annoying people, and people who give up on things halfway through. I want our world of fiction to be better than that.

There will be four players, including me. Once all four have signed up, no one else will be able to join. (Please

```
don't ask me how that works. My big brother is a computer
geek and he set up the site for me, but I don't know about
HTML or anything.)
```

Sawako was intrigued.

She'd gotten similar messages from "Yukari" before, which was odd because Sawako didn't remember giving her e-mail address to anyone with that name. She wondered if Yukari was for real. Was she really in junior high, or was she older? Maybe she wasn't even a "she."

Though Sawako loved reading and had often toyed with the idea of writing a story, she'd never been interested in the kinds of plots Yukari had suggested. One—about a quest to rescue a princess from a dragon—had been too childish, and another—about a school for witches—had struck her as a *Harry Potter* rip-off. But this one sounded more realistic, and the part about readers being frightened really appealed to Sawako. She wasn't into traditional horror stories about ghosts and vampires, but she did like a good psychological suspense tale.

```
Sawako, would you like to create a fictional world?
```

That line had won Sawako over. It was so much classier than if Yukari had written, "Sawako, want to join my role-playing game?" This wasn't a game, but a book written by four people. In the end, they would have something to show for their time: not fleeting text messages, but a real work of fiction.

Sawako remembered the first time she had come across the word "fictional," on a list of vocabulary words in her modern Japanese class in fourth grade.

Fictional stories, she had learned, were written so that they *seemed* real, kind of like a well-executed lie. *Fiction,* thought Sawako, *creates an unreal world that's better than the real one.*

The word and its definition had haunted her, although at the time she couldn't have explained why.

She sat down on the toilet seat to reread the e-mail.

"Good day to you, Taeko!"

"Oh, hi, Sae!"

The high-pitched voices of the girls who had come clattering in echoed against the cold, tiled walls of the bathroom. Even after they each entered a stall, they continued their all-important conversation. Chatter, chatter, chatter.

Annoyed at the interruption, Sawako punched in the site address Yukari had provided. The phone's net connection bar lengthened, and the screen quickly changed to the site for the story.

Despite Yukari's claim that her brother was a computer geek, the site was very plain. It was nothing more than a message board with a small window to enter your name into and a larger box where you could type your message. There were no graphics. The title said *Chain Mail* in pink letters, but the text below it was in blue font against a white screen.

```
Welcome to the fictional world.
    The heroine of our story is a girl in junior high school.
She's an only child from a wealthy family. She's not drop-
dead gorgeous, but she *is* pretty. She's also a kind, honest,
straightforward person. Even though she's mature in a lot of
ways, she still believes in "happily ever after" and that
one day her prince will come and rescue her.
    When the story begins, she has a boyfriend, and she
thinks that maybe *he's* her prince. He's a college student
who's been tutoring her at her home. Or maybe it would be
better if he isn't her boyfriend yet, but just a boy she
has a secret crush on. Either way, she really enjoys her
tutoring sessions.
    Then one day, the girl is walking home from school when
she sees a young man who's in some kind of trouble. Whoever
plays the heroine can decide what kind of situation he's in.
Anyway, she helps him out. He falls in love with her and
asks her to be his girlfriend. But she's in love with the
college guy, so she turns him down.
```

```
That man becomes her stalker.
There are four characters that you can play. Whoever
picks one gets to name him or her.

Heroine                                        (        )
Her tutor/boyfriend                            (        )
The woman detective who pursues the stalker    (        )
The stalker                                    (Yukari )

(I've already taken the role of the stalker. Sorry.)
If there's no name in the bracket by a character, you can
type in yours and choose that role. Once you've picked your
character, please write your part of the story in the box
below and hit "send" when you're done. I will write my part
after someone else begins the heroine's story.
See ya!
```

Sawako pondered over which role to choose. It didn't even occur to her not to play. She had no complaints about this story. *Too bad Yukari already took the stalker. Villains are always the most fun.*

The stalker would get to follow the heroine, ambush her, spy on her, make spooky phone calls, and send her threatening notes and packages and e-mails. He might even end up kidnapping her. Thinking about all the sick, perverted things he might do to prove his love sent an electric thrill of horror through Sawako's body.

But in the end, the stalker was just a creepy person doing creepy things. He might be imaginative, but he wasn't complicated. He only wanted one thing: for the heroine to love him. But the heroine could be complex. She was a good person who was about to go through a terrifying experience that would test her limits. She would have to become strong, and yet she wasn't the one driving the action—she could only react to what the stalker did. That must be so frustrating for her. So she'd be angry, and also sad and frightened. She'd cry and even despair, but she'd also figure out how to fight off the stalker.

And their duel would have to be as realistic as possible. Fiction made the unreal seem real.

The school bell chimed: five minutes to get to class. Sawako began to type.

Heroine   (Sawako)

She'd think some more about her character during class. Maybe she could even forward the e-mail to someone. They still needed a boyfriend and a detective. But she couldn't think of any friends who might want to play—or any friends at *all*, for that matter.

Still, who needed friends when you had a world of fiction to explore? Sawako picked up her bag and left the stall. For the first time since she came to this school, she caught the flash of her own smile in a mirror. Then another kind of flash caught her eye: silver against white.

Yuki Kanai's silver cell phone lay forgotten on the edge of the sink. Sawako didn't want to leave it, but she didn't want to turn it in to lost-and-found, either. Yuki was notorious. The teachers would be sure to use the opportunity to get Yuki in trouble, and then Kioi Academy's infamous bad girl would blame Sawako.

She decided to give the cell phone back. If her heroine was about to square off with a stalker, Sawako could get up the nerve to return a cell phone to another teenage girl. She picked it up. It was decorated with Donald Duck stickers—a funny choice for someone as tough as Yuki Kanai. Clutching the phone in her hand, Sawako ran down the cold stone hallway.

Mayumi
Friday, October 3, 9:28 pm.
Seibu-Shinjuku Line, Takadanobaba Station.

Tired commuters stood patiently on the platform, wedged tightly against each other in the post rush-hour crush. The doors to the express train slid open and then the crowd surged forward like a tidal wave.

"Hurry up, Sayuri!"

Mayumi rushed for two empty seats in the far corner. Holding her book bag and badminton racket close to her chest, she lunged butt-first for a seat. A middle-aged businessman was gunning for the seat next to her, but she slammed her racket down on top of it. Seizing Sayuri by the arm, Mayumi took away the racket and yanked her friend down to the seat in one smooth motion.

"Thanks, Mayumi," said Sayuri, settling in. She yawned. "I'm way too tired to stand all the way to Hon-Kawagoe."

The businessman muttered under his breath, something about kids and an easy life.

"Of course you're tired." Mayumi spoke loudly enough for the businessman to hear. "You got up at five and practiced at six, then you practiced on your lunch break, and then you practiced again from four to six-thirty this afternoon. You work even harder than a businessman."

The bitter look on the businessman's face deepened.

Mayumi continued, "And Coach Nakazawa was stricter than usual today. Did you notice him standing off to the side, glaring at us when we did those thirty sets? It made me so nervous, I felt like I was going to throw up."

Mayumi glanced at Sayuri, wondering if her friend was ever going to correct her on the "we" part. *Sayuri* had been the one who'd done the thirty sets, while Mayumi stood on the sidelines and stressed out on her behalf.

But Sayuri didn't seem to be listening. Instead, she was looking guiltily at the businessman. Then she shrugged. "Well, we got them first, so they're our seats."

"You're competing on a national level," Mayumi reasoned. "You deserve a seat. Seriously, Sayuri, I'm so proud of you. Hardly anyone goes national when they're still a freshman in junior high."

Sayuri sighed. "Yeah, but I don't have time for anything other than badminton. I have that test on equations tomorrow, but I'm too exhausted to study tonight."

"Want me to wake you up early tomorrow?" offered Mayumi. She pulled her cell phone from the blouse pocket of her uniform and thrust it at Sayuri. "Ta-da!"

"Ack!" yelped Sayuri, loudly enough that several passengers turned around. But since it was two junior high school girls squealing over a cell phone, the adults huffed in annoyance, then went back to their newspapers and magazines.

"What *is* that?" asked Sayuri, pushing the cell phone back at Mayumi. The screen displayed an eerie photo of a woman in a white kimono. Long, disheveled black hair hung over her face, hiding all of her features except for the glint of one eye.

"Oh, it's Sadako mail!" said Mayumi. "Haven't you seen it before?"

"What's 'Sadako mail'?"

"She's the spirit from that movie, *The Ring*. You know, the one with the cursed videotape. If you watch it, you die a week later, unless you can get someone else to watch it. Then they have to get someone else to see it, or else they'll die. Sadako mail is the e-mail version. If you don't forward it to seven people within twenty-four hours of opening it, you'll die."

"You better forward it quick, then," said Sayuri. "But not to me. It gives me the creeps."

"No way," scoffed Mayumi. "I'm not going to add to the amount of junk mail in the world."

The photo pulsed slightly. The screen now revealed a little bit more of Sadako's eye.

Sayuri peered at the subject line. "But look at all those forwards . . . A lot of people have passed it on. Doesn't it scare you just a little bit?"

"Nope!" Mayumi hit the delete key. The Sadako photo disappeared with a beep, replaced by a screensaver of Winnie the Pooh.

Sayuri gasped in horror, but Mayumi continued on, totally oblivious. "But I'll tell you what does scare me—the person who started it. I bet it's some creepy guy with no life and no girlfriend. I can picture him crouched in his tiny apartment, surrounded by hundreds of empty Cup of Noodles . . . all alone, late at night, getting off on the idea of scaring girls with his stupid prank e-mail . . . I can totally imagine him hunched over the keyboard, chuckling softly to himself . . ."

Sayuri shrank back into her seat. "Cut it out, Mayumi. You're freaking me out."

Mayumi laughed. "You're awake now, though, right?"

"Kinda."

"Then let's go over those equations." Ignoring Sayuri's ostentatious yawn, Mayumi pulled out her algebra textbook and opened it to the chapter on linear equations. "Let's start with the sample problem. There's an X on both sides, right? That means you need to move both Xs to the same side."

"Uh-huh."

Mayumi glanced at her friend to make sure she wasn't nodding off. "But when you move an X over the equal sign, its value changes. So this 5X becomes *negative* 5X, so the next step is . . ." She realized that she had no idea what the next step was. "Hang on. I'm not sure what to do about the parenthesis around the negative 3X. Let me think . . ." She chewed her lip. "Oh, I remember. It doesn't matter when you take away the parenthesis. Sayuri, you want to take it away first, or after we move the 5X . . . ? Sayuri?"

Sayuri's eyes were closed, and her head leaned against her racket as if it were a pillow. The skin of her cheek pressed through the mesh in tiny bulging squares.

The conductor's voice came through the loudspeaker. "We are now approaching Saginomiya. Next stop, Saginomiya."

The express train took exactly seven minutes to get from Takadanobaba to Saginomiya. It would have been enough time to solve a linear equation or two, but only if Mayumi hadn't wasted time teasing Sayuri about the Sadako mail. Though there was one more stop after Saginomiya, she hadn't the heart to wake her sleeping friend.

"Sorry about that," murmured Mayumi. She closed the textbook.

Sayuri was so pretty and vulnerable-looking as she slept, with her lips slightly parted and strands of black hair hanging over her face. Her head bobbed gently back and forth as the train swayed. Her new leather bag with "Nihon Joshi Academy" printed on it in big gold letters was slowly sliding off her lap. Mayumi gently took Sayuri's hand away from the handle, and put the bag in her own lap. Sayuri's palms were rough with calluses and half-healed blisters.

You keep on doing your best, Sayuri, thought Mayumi. *And if there's anything you can't keep hold of any more, I'll always be there to catch it for you.*

Mayumi couldn't remember a time when she hadn't been best friends with Sayuri. Their houses were on the same block. They'd gone to the same elementary school, and had been in the same class for all six years.

But they weren't the sort of friends who hung out together because it was convenient or because it was a childhood habit. They might have drifted into that sort of shallow relationship if their lives had gone differently, but one thing had transformed their friendship into an unbreakable bond: badminton.

They had joined the neighborhood badminton club when they were both ten. It was called the Tamagawa Waterworks Club and was nationally recognized. One of the four coaches was a former Olympic athlete, and club members regularly represented Tokyo in national competitions at the elementary school level.

The club had fifty members—both boys and girls from all six grades. Mayumi and Sayuri had only joined it because their parents had wanted them to get some exercise, but it quickly took over their lives. They trained every day after school and on every weekend that wasn't a holiday. They never got home before dark. Sometimes they had practice matches against adults who came by after work, and on those days the girls didn't get home until after eight.

Mayumi and Sayuri were together at school and at the club. They spent more time with each other than they did with their parents. But while badminton brought them together, it was also the one thing that kept them apart.

Sayuri turned out to be a natural athlete. She could run faster, jump higher, react quicker, and snap her wrists harder than any other girl her age. She hadn't even been in the club three months when she'd started practicing with the high school girls. She entered matches and the coaches put her in the same competitive bracket as girls several years older than her. She competed in the sixth grade bracket at the Tokyo City Tournament when she was in fourth and fifth grade, and won the gold medal both years.

After her second gold, she appeared on a TV variety show called "Genius Girl." The director asked her to hit a shuttlecock into the cheek of a comedian standing at the other end of the stage, and she hit it so accurately and with such force that they had to bleep out the comedian's response. The director was delighted.

Mayumi accompanied Sayuri to the set. She wished Sayuri luck, then stood in a dimly lit backstage corner, watching the bright lights shine down on her best friend.

Sure, maybe a lot of other girls would be jealous and angry to be overlooked, and they'd end up hating the friend who outshone them. But Mayumi had no resentment in her heart. She loved Sayuri, and she loved badminton. Or, to be precise, she loved the way that Sayuri played badminton.

Mayumi could stand at the edge of the court forever, watching Sayuri play. Her high clear shot that always fell just within bounds, her beautifully controlled hairpin shot that brushed over the net with less than an inch to spare, her powerful smash that crashed into the floor at more than a hundred kilometers per hour . . .

Mayumi never got as worked up when she played the game as when she watched Sayuri compete. It thrilled her to think that this primal force on the court was also her best friend.

It had quickly become clear that Mayumi would never be more than an average player and was not up to the standards of the Tamagawa Waterworks Club. But since the support staff were always underclassmen, Mayumi was able to volunteer for that position. She became Sayuri's right-hand girl. At every tournament, Mayumi was right behind her—a towel and a sports drink in hand.

When Sayuri was in sixth grade, one of Tokyo's best private schools, Nihon Joshi Academy, recruited her for their badminton team. In a moment of panic at the thought of being separated, Mayumi resolved that she would get accepted as well. But she was never going to get recruited for the team, and she hadn't bothered studying for entrance exams. She applied to a cram school, but it had a year-long program and they refused to admit her with only two months to go before the exam.

Mayumi didn't give up that easily. There was a girl in her class who had been studying with a famous cram school since the beginning of the year. She was supposed to be a brilliant student, so Mayumi asked if she'd mind doing a little coaching. They hadn't spoken before, but the girl agreed, and she coached Mayumi during lunch.

But as the cram school had told her, it was impossible to catch up on a year's worth of material in two months. Mayumi failed the exam. Desperate, she hatched wild plots to somehow get into Nihon Joshi anyway, including blackmailing the principal and hacking the records so it looked like she'd already been accepted.

Then suddenly her homeroom teacher called her into his office. "You've been accepted into Nihon Joshi," he informed her.

"But . . ." Mayumi barely stopped herself from blurting out that that was impossible.

Her teacher lowered his voice, even though they were alone in the office. "I'm going to tell you why, but you can't spread it around.

Apparently your friend Sayuri Sano said, 'If you don't accept Mayumi Hattori, I won't come either.' Nihon Joshi thinks Sano has Olympic potential, so they bent the rules for her."

Mayumi was overwhelmed by Sayuri's loyalty. "That's amazing! I can't wait to thank her!"

"Just a minute," he said. "They told me that Sano didn't want you to know that she's the reason you got in. But I know you, and I know if nobody told you why you'd been accepted, you'd keep asking and investigating until you figured it out. But do me a favor and don't tell Sano I told you, okay?"

Mayumi never revealed that she knew how Sayuri had stood up for her. She figured that Sayuri must have been embarrassed by the strength of her feelings, or maybe Sayuri thought Mayumi would be happier if she believed that she'd gotten in on her own merits. But Mayumi didn't care why Nihon Joshi had let her in, as long as she could stay with Sayuri.

So for the last six months, Mayumi had carried a racket case emblazoned with "Nihon Joshi" in gold, and had stood on the sidelines and watched Sayuri dominate the junior high and intramural tournaments. It had been a once-in-a-lifetime experience, and it was all thanks to Sayuri. So Mayumi decided to become a pillar of strength for Sayuri to lean on.

And Sayuri needed her support. Though the good times were blazingly good, their schedule was so tough that the boring and painful times usually outnumbered the fun ones.

Mayumi kept the same schedule as Sayuri, including the lunchtime and afternoon training sessions, which meant that both of them woke up at four thirty or five to get to practice by six. They spent an hour and a half commuting on the Seibu Shinjuku train line and the Touzai subway line, and they rarely got home before ten. Sayuri was so exhausted from practicing that she slept instead of studying, and though she'd recently made it to the third round of the city badminton finals, her grades were the worst in her class.

Mayumi's were the second worst. Although she never took her racket out of its case, all her energy was directed toward supporting Sayuri. She gathered up the shuttlecocks, waited on the sidelines with a towel and a cold bottle of her favorite sports drink, Pocari Sweat, and cheered Sayuri on. She was content with that. But she was tired, too.

Sayuri shifted in her sleep so that her head rested on Mayumi's shoulder. Mayumi lowered her head and briefly brushed Sayuri's soft cheek with her own.

Not everyone can be the hero of their own story, thought Mayumi. *Even a star like Sayuri can't shine all by herself, without any help from people like me.*

"We are now approaching Kamishakujii," announced the conductor. "Next stop, Kamishakujii."

Mayumi looked out the opposite window, careful not to disturb Sayuri's sleep. The city flowed by, a river of darkness speckled with sparkling lights.

It took exactly ten minutes to get from Kamishakujii to Kodaira. Mayumi decided to e-mail her house. Because the girls got home so late, their parents took turns picking them up from the station. Tonight was Mayumi's family's turn.

She flipped open her cell phone and was about to hit "compose" when she noticed that she had a new message from an address she didn't recognize. *Probably more spam like the Sadako mail*, she thought. Mayumi opened the message.

OCTOBER 3, 7:35 PM
SUBJECT: MAYUMI, WOULD YOU LIKE TO CREATE A FICTIONAL WORLD?

Hi, I'm Sawako. I'm a girl (obviously), and a freshman at a private junior high school in Tokyo. I got this e-mail, and it seemed interesting—really, it's not a boring spam message—so I'm forwarding it to you.

FW: Hi. My name is Yukari. In case you can't tell from my name, I'm a girl. I'm a freshman at a private junior high school in Tokyo.

I'm sick of a lot of things. Aren't you? Like parents who keep nagging you to study, or the teachers who just act like glorified babysitters. But the people who piss me off the most are my so-called friends.

Mayumi wasn't sure who Sawako was or how the girl had known her e-mail address, but Sawako had been right to think that Mayumi would be interested in the message. It wasn't the teen angst stuff about nagging parents and pointless chatter that intrigued Mayumi, but the idea of writing a thriller.

Last year, during a long, dull weekend afternoon, Mayumi had wandered into her father's room and picked up one of his stashes of paperback Agatha Christie murder mysteries. She was instantly enthralled. Her father was into foreign mysteries, mostly from America and England, and he and Mayumi soon began to trade their favorite titles in that genre.

Though she still liked Christie's intellectual detective Hercules Poirot, she came to prefer tougher protagonists, like Michael Connelly's lone-wolf detective, Harry Bosch, or even criminals like Thomas Harris' Hannibal Lector. Her favorite author was Patricia Highsmith. All the characters in her novels had warped personalities; some were smooth and cunning sociopaths who plotted clever crimes and got away with them.

No matter the plot, Mayumi was always thrilled by the tales of desperation and evil.

She hadn't had much time to read this year, but she did manage to get a little bit in while riding the train to and from school. Sayuri tended to fall asleep, but since Mayumi didn't spend hours exercising, she usually had enough energy to read a couple chapters.

But her father was the only person she could talk to about her passion for fictional mayhem. She wished she could chat about it with girls her own age, but Sayuri wasn't much of a reader, and Mayumi worried that other girls at school would be freaked out if she said things like, "And then Doctor Lector eats the man's liver with fava beans and a nice Chianti," or, "It was so exciting when Tom Ripley murdered his friend on the boat."

So Mayumi was delighted to hear from another girl who also liked thrillers. She felt like she was already Yukari's friend.

Actually, it sounds like she could teach me some things about mysteries, thought Mayumi. *She came up with a great story. I'd love to write the part of the heroine . . . though Yukari might have taken that already.*

Then one day, the girl is walking home from school when she sees a young man who's in some kind of trouble. Whoever plays the heroine can decide what kind of situation he's in. Anyway, she helps him out. He falls in love with her and asks her to be his girlfriend. But she's in love with the college student, so she turns him down.

That man becomes her stalker.

On second thought, I'd rather be the stalker, thought Mayumi. Then she reached the end of the page:

Heroine	(Sawako)
Her tutor/boyfriend	(·)
The woman detective who pursues the stalker	( )
The stalker	(Yukari)

"Wha—?!" Mayumi exclaimed aloud. Both of the best parts had already been taken!

But she had no intention of not signing up. She loved the idea of writing her own crime novel, and she was determined to play a character in this one.

In a thriller, like the ones by Patricia Highsmith or Barbara Michaels, the main character was either the villain or the person the villain stalked. But in a traditional mystery, like one of Agatha Christie's or Michael Connelly's, the hero was the detective.

There're only four characters in this story, thought Mayumi. *Any one of them could end up being the main character.*

Mayumi was seized with the horrible notion that this message could have been forwarded all over Tokyo, and *right that second* some other girl could be thinking the same thing she was. She quickly moved her cursor to the space beside "The woman detective who pursues the stalker," wrote in her own name, and hit "enter."

To her relief, her own name appeared when the page refreshed.

Now all I have to do is figure out how to make myself the real hero of the story. Feeling proud of herself for managing to snag the plum role, Mayumi was about to close the cell phone when a new line of text appeared on the screen:

One new entry.

It's already started! she thought excitedly.

DATE AND TIME: OCTOBER 3, 12:27 PM
AUTHOR: SAWAKO
CHARACTER: SAWAKO SHINODA

Someone is watching me.

It started about a month ago. At first I thought I was imagining things. But no matter where I went (unless I was home or in a room without windows) the skin on my back would start to prickle. I'd keep rubbing the back of my neck. My shoulders would quiver and shift, and finally I'd have to turn around and look . . . but there was never anyone there.

It happened when I left home, on the train to school, and when I went on the field for gym class. Finally I told my father. At first he listened carefully and really seemed concerned for me. But then he gave me a talk about how all girls start to feel self-conscious when they become teenagers, and that I had to remember that the only person remotely interested in me was me.

I said it wasn't like that and that I really believed that someone was watching me. Then he got a funny look on his face—half-worried and half-disgusted—and told me that I must be overly tired and to go on to bed. Just so you know, when you talk about scary things, people start to think that *you're* the one who's scary. I swear that I'm not making any of this up.

I felt that gaze on me again today as I walked back from cram school along the banks of Meguro River. The river is on one side, and on the other side is a huge wall around a construction zone. The path isn't wide enough for two people to walk side by side, so if there was someone else on it, they were either in front of me or behind me. The path curves, so it's hard to see, but it straightened out up ahead, and I didn't see anyone else.

Which meant . . .

I looked over my shoulder. No one was there. Maybe the *suggestion* of a shadow or a movement that had stopped just as I'd turned around?

I started to run. If anyone saw me, they'd think I was crazy: a schoolgirl clutching her book bag and fleeing headlong from nobody. But I didn't care. The path didn't feel safe anymore, not with sensation of being watched and feeling trapped by the deep river beside me.

I soon came within sight of the bridge that led to a bus path. At that point, I decided to forget about my daily exercise, and just take the bus back home. I bolted onto the bridge, relieved to leave the river path behind.

"Hello," came a voice from behind me.

I screamed and spun around. A young man stood at the base of the bridge; he smiled at me. He didn't seem at all surprised or worried that I'd screamed. He was tall and lanky, and was wearing a worn-out green polo shirt, jeans with holes in the knees, and a ratty gray jacket. His hair was long and looked slick—not stiff and shiny as if he'd merely used too much gel, but greasy as if he never washed it. But as I stared at him in horror, I began to remember those evasive eyes behind his speckled glasses.

"I know you," I said. "You're that guy . . ."

His smile widened "I knew you'd remember!"

About a month ago, I'd been walking along the river when I saw him crouching in the middle of the path, doubled over in pain. There was no one else around and I couldn't get him to say anything coherent, so I used my cell phone to call an ambulance.

"I had appendicitis," he explained. "They had to rush me into surgery. They told me later that if you hadn't called an ambulance, my appendix would have burst, and I could have gotten peritonitis and died." He stroked his patchy stubble as he spoke.

I didn't know what to say. It made sense that he'd be grateful to me, but something about him made me uncomfortable. Maybe it was the strange tone in his voice as he said words like "peritonitis" and "died." It almost sounded like relish.

"That's . . . good," I said awkwardly.

"So you saved my life!" he said gleefully. "And now I get to thank you!"

"You're welcome," I said, edging a step back.

"I'm so rude," he said. "I never introduced myself. I'm Tetsuro Tsunoda."

"Sawako Shinoda," I replied automatically, then wished I hadn't.

"Sawako," he said slowly, as if caressing my name with his tongue. "I've been wondering what your name was." He took a step toward me. "Sawako is even prettier than the names I've been imagining."

Before I could make an excuse and get away, he pulled two tickets from his pocket and held them out like a fan. "So here's my thank you: two tickets to the opera. It's Verdi's *Rigoletto* by the Bologna Opera Troupe. This is their only stop in Japan, so it's a very special treat. Box seats, of course."

"You don't need to do anything special to thank me," I said. "I'm just happy you're all right now." By then I was wishing I'd left him alone with his bursting appendix, but I was so used to being polite to strangers that the proper words came out of my mouth of their own accord. "Anyway, I don't know anything about opera."

"You don't need to," he said. *"Rigoletto* is very simple. It's about love and passion, and I'm sure you know all about that. I'm just glad I could catch you. I meant to give these to you yesterday, but you took the day off cram school, and I wasn't sure where you were. I'm so happy you came back today, because the tickets are for tomorrow night."

I got that itchy feeling on the back of my neck again. "How do you know I skipped class last week?"

"You didn't walk along the river last week, and you only seem to come this way when you go to your cram school on Thursday. Your class is from five to seven, right? It must be, because you pass the bridge at four forty-five on your way there, and at seven-fifteen on your way back."

He winked, as if inviting me to share in his cleverness, and then he tugged at the collar of his jacket. It fell open, revealing a pair of binoculars.

Though the night was cool, I felt a bead of sweat roll down my back.

"I've noticed that not many people walk this way," Tsunoda said, picking the binoculars up. "So I thought it would be a nice, private place to talk to you, Sawako."

"So you waited for me here last week?" I tried not to let my voice shake, but it did anyway.

He nodded. "But you never came. So I pinned my hopes on today. But don't worry! If you hadn't come today, I would have caught you tomorrow morning at the train station. Ikejiri-oohashi station, the express train to Oshiage, second door of the third car. Right?"

I opened my mouth to ask him how he knew, but my tongue felt like a wad of cotton. Anyway, I already knew the answer. I glanced at the binoculars hanging around his neck.

Run now, Sawako, I ordered myself. *Before it's too late.*

I took a step, but I was so shaky that I tripped myself.

"Steady there." Tsunoda caught my arm. His palm was soft and damp, like a huge maggot. I flinched away.

"I'm sorry," I said automatically.

Then I came to my senses and ran. The hot September wind pulled at my hair, reminding me of the heat of his sticky fingers.

"Tomorrow night at six!" Tsunoda yelled after me.

I glanced over my shoulder. He stood there smiling, as if there was nothing unusual about girls running away from him. The wind carried his voice to me. "In front of the Ueno Culture Hall! I'll be waiting!"

"That was cool!" exclaimed Mayumi. She only realized that she had spoken aloud when everyone on the train who wasn't asleep or wearing headphones turned to look at her. But she didn't care.

She loved the way the stalker had been introduced. The suddenness of his appearance and the way he seemed to have no idea that he might be scaring Sawako had been wonderfully eerie. Whoever Sawako was, she was a good writer. It was a little weird that she had named her character after herself, but who cared when she could write such a great stalker? *But I bet I could do even better.*

Mayumi couldn't wait to read what would happen next between Tsunoda and Sawako Shinoda. And she was dying to start writing for her own character.

She hadn't decided yet, but she thought it would probably be more realistic to have her detective be a cop rather than a private eye—a cop who would take the call when Sawako Shinoda first reported her stalker, and might get personally involved later on.

Sawako, quick, call the police! Mayumi prayed.

"We are now approaching Kodaira. Next stop, Kodaira," intoned the conductor.

It wouldn't be long now before Mayumi was in bed, but she didn't think she'd get much sleep tonight.

MAI
FRIDAY, OCTOBER 3, 9:53 PM.
SEIYU DEPARTMENT STORE, TAKADANOBABA BRANCH.

When Mai left the concert hall, a light drizzle was falling. Few cars were on the glistening streets and the sidewalk was littered with discarded plastic bags. Mai tried to let the post-concert exhilaration warm her, but a chill began to seep in.

"You going home already?" inquired someone behind her.

Five high school girls were squatting by the backstage exit. They all held their hands or hats or umbrellas over their cigarettes to keep the rain from putting them out. Mai remembered them from the front row of the Chaos Mode concert, standing up and bobbing their heads in unison.

"They'll all be coming out soon," said a girl in leather pants and a mesh T-shirt.

"Who's your favorite?" asked a girl with purple hair. "I am madly in love with Ryota, because guitarists are the best and I have good taste."

The tall girl who had spoken to Mai now addressed the purple-haired girl. "You ever think maybe other people have their own opinions? You are so self-centered, Mari . . . even if you *do* have good taste." This seemed to be a running joke, because all five of the girls started to laugh. The smoke from their cigarettes eddied up against a sign by the exit that read: *Please do not wait for the performers here.*

"I'm not interested in meeting the band," said Mai. Her words were so cool and abrupt that the girls stopped laughing. "I don't care what they're like as people, and I don't want to be their buddy. All I'm interested in is the music."

Mai started to walk past them.

"What I'm interested in is: who put the stick up your ass?" jeered the girl wearing leather pants.

"Rich bitch junior high school brat," said Mari. "We had to work to get the money for the concert, but her parents just hand it over every time she goes whining to them for more."

The tall girl looked uncomfortable. "Cut it out, you guys."

"Run back to Mommy, you little baby!" yelled a girl wearing a slinky, gold lamé dress. "Run and tell her you want to go back to New York City."

She stopped and looked back. Mai didn't recognize any of them, but obviously the girl knew her.

"You do, don't you?" said the gold lamé girl. "I know all about you. Your daddy's with the Ministry of Foreign Affairs and your mommy thinks you walk on water. 'In America you get your driver's license when you're sixteen,'" she said in an affected tone that, to Mai's fury, was a dead-on parody of her mother's voice. "'In America, a third year junior high school student is treated just like an adult. So my baby Mai is really all grown up now.'"

"How do you know all this stuff?" demanded Mai.

The girl smiled. "Groupies know everything. For instance, we know that schools make special allowances for kids who come back from spending years overseas. That, plus your daddy's job are the only reasons you got into your fancy school, because everyone knows kids in America don't study."

The leather-pants girl said, "You should talk, Minori. You don't study either."

All the girls but Minori started laughing again.

Minori hissed. "So shut up about your 'I don't care about the band.' Who do you think you are? You think you come from a better place than we do, like we're some kind of hillbillies compared to you?"

Mai hurried away before Minori could say anything else. She could feel her face going hot with a rush of blood, but she kept her head low as she went by so the girls wouldn't mock her blush too. She was so upset that it took her several minutes to remember to put up her umbrella, and as a result, the leather jacket she'd bought in New York got wet.

Minori had been right about Mai's mother. Whenever the other mothers in the neighborhood complained about their kids, Mai's mother would spout out some piece of American wisdom, like, "You should be happy if your daughters have a boyfriend. In America parents aren't at all embarrassed or worried when their children start dating." Or, "I learned in America that if you trust your kids and treat them like adults, they'll live up to your expectations. So I'm not at all concerned when Mai goes to clubs, because she's a big girl now and she knows how to behave."

Mai suspected that her mother *did* worry about her going to clubs, but was afraid that saying so would ruin her cosmopolitan image. It frustrated Mai that her mother let her do whatever she wanted, regardless of how her mother really felt about it, just in order to prove how enlightened and liberal she was. Mai would have actually preferred some honest discipline.

"Dammit!" muttered Mai aloud as she stomped down Waseda Street. "Everything pisses me off." She reached into the pocket of her parachute pants for her iPod. No matter how much the world sucked, Black Thunder could always comfort her.

Black Thunder was an indie J-rock band that hadn't yet been discovered by the mainstream media, or the so-called fans who cared more about the drummer's sexiness than the actual music. They had only released one CD so far, but they played live on a regular basis. Though the CD was great, it was their live shows that set them apart. Their sets, costumes, and makeup—and most of all, their music—created a dark and beautiful fantasy world.

Let me leave this boring life behind, thought Mai.

Mai's hand didn't touch her iPod, but rather her cell phone. While still daydreaming about Black Thunder, she automatically pulled it out and opened it. Realizing what she had done, she chuckled to herself. *Might as well check their schedule. Maybe they've got some new bookings.*

Then she noticed the envelope icon. She had an e-mail.

She wondered who it was from. She didn't chat much online. Despite her tough exterior, she got self-conscious when she had to write her thoughts down.

She always imagined her words being read and reread and scrutinized. So when people e-mailed her to say, "What are you doing?" she'd imagine writing, "I'm alive," or, "I'm breathing," and then decided that those replies were too weird. Then she'd imagine writing what they probably expected, which was, "Oh, nothing— what are you doing?" but that was so trite. Mai usually ended up not replying at all.

She didn't recognize the sender, but it didn't look like spam. She opened the message.

OCTOBER 3, 7:37 PM
SUBJECT: MAI, WOULD YOU LIKE TO CREATE A FICTIONAL WORLD?

Hi, I'm Sawako. I'm a girl (obviously) and a first year student at a private junior high school in Tokyo. I got this e-mail, and it seemed interesting—really, it's not a boring spam message—so I'm forwarding it to you.

FW: Hi. My name is Yukari. In case you can't tell from my name, I'm a girl. I'm a freshman at a private junior high school in Tokyo.

I'm sick of a lot of things. Aren't you? Like parents who keep nagging you to study, or the teachers who just act like glorified babysitters. But the people who piss me off the most are my so-called friends.

The story sounded interesting, but it was Yukari's opening rant that caught Mai's attention. She agreed with everything Yukari said about tedious chitchat, fair-weather friends, and the bitchy, shallow social scene at school. Mai *was* sick of a lot of things. She felt liberated by reading the words Yukari had written. At least one other girl felt the same way Mai did. Maybe she was no longer alone.

A train roared down the overpass of Takadanobaba station. Mai leaned against the wall of a bank, rereading her favorite parts of the message. Below the overpass, a college-aged couple snuggled while a drunken businessman squatted with his head in his hands. Mai ignored them, lost in the message.

She would have considered anything Yukari proposed, but Mai actually did like the idea of writing a story. She loved being swept into the world of Black Thunder . . . *Why not create my own world that would sweep in other people? Why not a world where I'm in charge?* She smiled at the thought.

There was only one role left to play, but since she had never written a story before, she didn't have a lot invested in wanting a particular part. She entered her own name beside the listing for "the heroine's boyfriend/tutor," then checked the message board.

There were two entries. The first was by Sawako, and told how Sawako Shinoda met her stalker, Tsunoda. The second entry, by Yukari, was about the stalker.

DATE AND TIME: OCTOBER 3, 4:37 PM
AUTHOR: YUKARI
CHARACTER: TETSURO TSUNODA
    Sawako. What a beautiful name. I'm sure she'll meet me for the opera. The fact that she ran away proves that she liked me. She was overwhelmed by her feelings, so she ran.
    You see it all the time on TV. A man proposes to the woman he loves. She's so happy that she can't even say yes, and instead, she runs away. The man stands there, dumbstruck, thinking she's turned him down. And then, with tears streaming down her smiling face, she returns to him.
    Sawako acted just like that with me. I bet she'll be smiling through her tears when she comes to me tomorrow.

She really loves me. Yukio was wrong about her. Yukio's an old friend of mine. I'd told him about Sawako before I even knew her name. "I've finally found her," I'd said. "I've found the angel I've been looking for my entire life—the woman who will complete me. I've been watching her for weeks now, and I'm sure she's the one. I memorized her schedule, and when she goes by Meguro Bridge this Thursday, I'll introduce myself and ask her out."

Yukio'd looked worried. He'd said, "Don't do that, Tetsuro. It's illegal and wrong."

But look at how well it worked out. Sawako was thrilled.

Anyway, what does "wrong" mean? Who decides what's wrong and what's right? How can doing what your lover wants be wrong? How can it be wrong to make her happy?

It's possible—not likely, but possible—that Sawako was only pretending to be happy. But even if she wasn't truly delighted to meet me, I still did the right thing.

That's because right and wrong aren't determined by personal happiness. It isn't the person who benefits from a good deed that determines its worth, but rather it all depends on the quality of the person doing the deed.

For instance, I hate studying. Reading bores me and math is a struggle. But my homeroom teacher forced me to study. He told me that reading and math were vital skills, and that I would never succeed in life if I couldn't master the basics. He said, "Whether you like them or not, they're good things to know." He was right.

I hate carrots. They smell like dirt and I don't like the sinewy parts that get stuck between my teeth. But my mother always told me, "It doesn't matter whether you like them or not. You have to eat carrots because they're good for you." And she was right.

So you see, it was my homeroom teacher who decided that studying was good, and my mother who decided that carrots were good. My feelings on the subject didn't matter at all.

That's why it's right for me to be Sawako's guardian angel, and never stop watching over her.

"This is great!" exclaimed Mai.

Another businessman blinked sleepily at her. While engrossed in the story, she had walked to the train station and boarded the train. She'd been so caught up in the story that she worried she'd missed her stop. To her relief, the train had only just left Shin Okubo station. The rain blurred the bright signs of Kabukicho outside. The neon lights flashed quickly, but not as quickly as the beating of Mai's heart.

Chain Mail was nothing but a story created by teenage girls just like herself, and yet it transcended reality as easily as Black Thunder's music.

I've got to do this, thought Mai. *I've got to create my own story.*

II.

"At times one remains faithful to a cause
only because its opponents do not cease
to be insipid."

NIETZSCHE
BEYOND GOOD AND EVIL

DATE AND TIME: OCTOBER 4, 9:19 AM
AUTHOR: MAI
CHARACTER: KOUHEI KIMURA

I knocked on the door of Sawako's house.

I tutor her every week in English and Math. She's about to take the high school entrance exams.

Before her mother could finish saying, "Mister Kimura is here," Sawako had flown down the stairs. I don't ever remember being that happy to see my tutor when I was in junior high, but Sawako's always delighted at the thought of a study session. She grabbed my hand and dragged me up the stairs, jumping up two steps at a time.

"I'll bring up some tea later!" Mrs. Shinoda called up the stairs.

"There're so many things I don't understand," Sawako told me cheerfully. "And I expect you to explain every single one of them."

Her room was bigger than that of any other child I tutor. She had a nice desk under a window that looked out to the street, and queen-sized bed against the wall. A shelf over the bed held Disney movie figurines—not the new ones, but from older films like *Cinderella* and

Sleeping Beauty. There was a low table in the middle that was bigger than a normal house's dining room table. But the room was so big that none of the furniture was crowded together. You could have had a wrestling match in the empty space.

Notebooks and study guides were spread over the low table. And hidden under one of the study guides, but recognizable by its red cover, was our "Secret Notebook."

Sawako's mother always made us keep the door open, so she could hear what we were doing from downstairs. I guess it made her nervous that Sawako was alone with me, when she was fifteen and a third year junior high school student, and I was eighteen and in college. But knowing that she was listening made me feel uncomfortable with saying anything that wasn't directly related to Sawako's studies, even if it was totally innocent.

But Sawako got bored just doing problems and nothing else for two hours straight, so she had created the Secret Notebook. While I taught her, if she felt like chatting a bit, she'd write her thoughts in the notebook, and then I'd write my replies there. Even if her mother came up the stairs and peeked in on us, it would just look like we were writing down problems.

At first I thought the lack of trust and communication between Sawako and her mother was weird, but after three months of tutoring, I got used to it. But I was a little disturbed by some of the questions Sawako wrote in the Secret Notebook. Like, *Do you have a girlfriend, Kouhei?*

She'd written that a month ago. When I replied that I didn't, it seemed to open the floodgates: *What's your favorite color? Do you like it better when girls wear jeans or skirts? What kind of girls do you like?*

I tried to write back answers that didn't seem like flirting, but it was becoming pretty clear that Sawako thought of me as more than just a tutor.

Sure, she was cute. Physically mature—and tall for her age. When she put on dark lipstick and wore regular clothes instead of her school uniform, she could have passed for a college student.

But there's a big gap between junior high and high school, let alone junior high and college. A fifteen-year-old is still just a child. I don't date children, and I didn't know how to deal with the crush of a fifteen-year-old.

Congratulations on winning the tournament yesterday! she wrote.

I was surprised that she knew about that.

You came? I wrote.

Yeah. I watched the whole thing from the first round.

It had been an intercollegiate tournament, and I'd won in the sixth round for my university tennis club.

Why didn't you say hello afterward?

She paused, then wrote, *You were with a pretty girl the whole time, Kouhei. I felt like I'd be butting in. Is she your girlfriend?*

I sighed. *No, she's in the club too. I told you, I don't have a girlfriend.*

Really? Okay, I believe you. But when you do get one, I just might have to get in her way. Sawako looked up from the notebook with a playful smile.

I decided to change the subject. "Oh, yeah." I was so flustered that I spoke aloud. "When I got here, there was a guy standing outside. Is he a friend of yours? He was looking up at your window."

The flirtatious look dropped from Sawako's face. Without a word, she walked to the window and peeked through the curtains. Whatever she saw outside made her jerk away from the window as if the glass was hot enough to burn her.

"What's the matter?" I came up beside her and looked outside.

That young man I'd seen before was still there. But now he was watching the house through a pair of binoculars.

Sawako grabbed my arm and pulled me away. In whispers, she told me how she'd called an ambulance for that man and how he'd accosted her later at Meguro River. As soon as she finished her story, I ran downstairs and threw the front door open.

No one was there.

```
DATE AND TIME: OCTOBER 4, 5:37 PM
AUTHOR: YUKARI
CHARACTER: TETSURO TSUNODA
    Who is that guy?
    Who is that guy who visits my Sawako's house once a week
and even goes inside her bedroom?
    He always brings books, so maybe he's her tutor. But she
stood me up last night, and went to watch him play tennis
instead. There's no way their relationship is just tutor/
student.
    There's something wrong with Sawako if she'd pass up a
date with me at the opera to watch that college boy play
games.
    No, it's not her fault. It's his. He's a bad influence.
    Bad boys need to be punished.
```

DATE AND TIME: OCTOBER 5, 12:59 AM
AUTHOR: SAWAKO
CHARACTER: SAWAKO SHINODA

Yesterday something awful happened. Mama fired Kouhei.

"Why?!" I yelled.

"It wasn't a good idea to hire a man in college to tutor a girl your age. I called the tutoring center, and they'll send a woman to tutor you from now on."

I couldn't believe it. "What do you think Kouhei was doing?!"

" 'Kouhei,' huh?" said Mama. "Is that what you call Mister Kimura? It sounds like I did the right thing."

"What are you talking about?" I asked. "Sure, we called each other by our first names, but it was just a friendly thing. Why can't you trust me?

I've always been a good daughter. I never ask for anything. Come on, tell them to send him back."

"I can't do that," Mama said. "Believe me, it's for your own good. A girl your age is full of dreams, and you can't tell the difference between fantasy and reality. You get an idea of what a person's like, and then you put that image on a pedestal. Your Mister Kimura isn't the prince you think he is."

"How would *you* know?" I demanded.

"I just do. Now, your new tutor is a graduate student at Ochanomizu University, and—"

I cut her off. "If Kouhei can't tutor me, I'm not going to study!"

"Sawako!"

I turned my back to her and ran up to my room.

```
DATE AND TIME: OCTOBER 5, 9:29 AM
AUTHOR: YUKARI
CHARACTER: TETSURO TSUNODA
```

Yesterday I caught Sawako again at the bridge over Meguro River. It wasn't the same bridge as last week, but a different one that's closer to the train station.

Sawako isn't as smart as she thinks she is. Or maybe she *wanted* me to catch her. She changed her route to cram school, but she didn't avoid the river entirely.

She appeared at 5:17 in the evening, looking distracted—as if she was thinking hard about something or someone other than me. I didn't like that. She wore blue jeans and a pink T-shirt with cute red fringe around the collar and sleeves.

"Hello." I stepped out of the shadow of the bridge. From the look on Sawako's face, she was thinking about me *now*.

"You stood me up last week. I waited for you for so long that I missed the concert."

"I told you I wasn't going to come."

"No, that wasn't what you said, Sawako. You said that you didn't know anything about opera and I told you that it didn't matter."

Sawako flinched. Oops, I must have let her see that I was angry.

"But you're free this Sunday, right? I bought two more tickets. This one is for Suntory Hall. It's Vivaldi's *The Four Seasons*. I'm sure you know some of the songs already. And it's a very accessible piece, even if you're not into classical music."

"I have plans this Sunday." Sawako's voice was thick, as if her tongue had gone stiff.

"What plans?"

She looked around.

"I-I'm going to watch a friend at a tennis tournament."

"Wasn't that last week?" I asked.

Sawako's eyes opened wide. "How did you know that?"

"Besides, Mister Kimura isn't your tutor any more, right?"

Sawako stood there, staring at me. Her black eyes were as pure as the night sky and her rage made them shine like stars.

"It was you, wasn't it?" Sawako's lips twisted with fury, but her anger only made her more beautiful. "You told my mother lies about Kouhei. You made her fire him, didn't you? What did you tell her? Did you say you were a classmate of his?"

"It was for your own good," I explained. "He seemed to be distracting you from your studies. You'll never succeed in life if you don't master the basics."

"What do *you* care?!" exploded Sawako. "You never had appendicitis, did you? You pretended to be sick just to have an excuse to get near me, didn't you?"

"That's not true," I said soothingly. "If I'd wanted to—"

"You stay away from me!" she shrieked. "What you're doing is called stalking! Do you understand? You're a pervert!"

And with that sudden outburst, she ran away.

"Sunday at five, Sawako!" I called after her. "Suntory Hall! Don't forget!"

"You're crazy!" yelled Sawako without turning around. "I'm not going anywhere with you!"

An old woman clutching a shopping bag looked first at Sawako, then at me. She shook her head at me like she thought I was an idiot. But when I glared back at her, she turned away and hurried along like I'd scared her.

Sawako doesn't understand. I have to educate her. It's a man's job to explain the ways of the world to the woman he loves. Sawako might not enjoy it, but it's something she needs.

The person who decides what's right is the person who does the good deed.

SAWAKO

MONDAY, OCTOBER 6, 3:43 PM.

AT THE MAIN GATE OF KIOI ACADEMY.

Sawako dashed through the gates of Kioi Academy. The instant she was outside, she pulled out her cell phone and connected to the Internet. The *Chain Mail* website came up immediately. Since it was always the first thing she checked, she'd reset it as her homepage.

The story had progressed quickly over the weekend. Yukari had taken Tsunoda, whom Sawako had first named and described, and breathed life into him. Mai had created the tutor, Kouhei Kimura, and set up a juicy conflict between Sawako Shinoda's crush on him and his belief that she was only a kid, and further moved the action forward by having him attempt to confront Tsunoda.

As Sawako reread the last entry, the sound of a hymn rose above the noises of gossiping girls and pattering feet.

"Come, ye souls by sin afflicted, bowed with fruitless sorrow down; by the broken law convicted, through the cross behold the crown; look to Jesus; mercy flows through him alone . . ."

It was the Kioi Academy Choir. Though the majority of the students weren't Christian, Kioi Academy was a mission school and had a small chapel on its grounds, built in the same forbidding style as the main building.

The lyrics of the hymn intrigued her. According to Christians, God, the father of Jesus, was the creator of the world. But Sawako, Yukari, Mai, and Mayumi were the creators of the *Chain Mail* world—a world contained in their cell phones. Their world was completely separate from the one that God created, which was full of boring and ugly things. In the world the girls created with their fingertips, Sawako, Tsunoda, and Kouhei struggled and suffered, "bowed by fruitless sorrow down."

I wonder what sort of ordeals I should put them through today?

"Hey, you."

Even before Sawako turned around, she recognized the voice as Yuki Kanai's. When she did turn, she saw that Yuki was wearing a filmy blue camisole and barely-there denim short-shorts—an outrageous outfit, even considering Kioi's liberal dress code. Only Yuki would wear such a thing to school. She had dyed her long hair chestnut brown since the last time Sawako had seen her.

"Yes?" Sawako took a step backward. Apart from Yuki's reputation as Kioi Academy's bad girl, something about the way she was eyeing Sawako made her nervous.

"Why are you looking at your cell phone?" Yuki was wearing so much mascara and blue eye shadow that she looked like she'd recently been punched in both eyes, but her gaze was keen.

"No reason."

"Are you sending an e-mail?" Yuki leaned over and tried to peek at the screen. Sawako put the phone behind her back, then closed it.

"Guess a girl's got to have her secrets," said Yuki. "Listen, we met in the bathroom last Friday before school, right?"

Sawako felt a muscle in her cheek twitch with anxiety, but she didn't reply.

"Did I leave my cell phone by the sink?" asked Yuki.

Sawako shook her head.

"Really? That's weird." Yuki pursed her lips, which were painted blood-red and outlined in black, in honor of her current sex-kitten-meets-juvenile-delinquent look. "Well, I *did* leave my phone there. But when I went back to get it after first period, it was gone. So I thought you might have taken it to give back to me. But then a girl brought it to me at lunch. She said she'd just found it. And when I asked where, she said, 'On the sink.'"

Sawako wasn't looking at Yuki as the other girl spoke, so she noticed the reactions of the other students as they walked around the two of them. Their gaze slid right off Sawako like she wasn't there, but when they recognized Yuki, the school's number one troublemaker, their faces registered fear and respect, and then they hurried away.

"Don't you think that's strange?" asked Yuki. "You said the phone wasn't there. I went back to look for it, and I didn't see it anywhere. But the other girl said she found it at lunch, on the sink. It wouldn't have stayed there for three periods without someone picking it up, so what I'm wondering is, where was it all morning?"

Sawako stared at the asphalt beneath her feet. "I don't know."

"Are you sure about that?"

Sawako clenched her jaw, then looked up. "Are you accusing me of something?"

"Hey, Sawako!" Both girls turned toward the man's voice.

"Whoops, here comes Sakata." Yuki clicked her tongue and ran off.

As Yuki disappeared around the corner, Sawako's homeroom teacher came up. Mister Sakata was a young teacher who'd only graduated from college three years ago. He used to play rugby, and the buttons on his dress shirt always looked like they were going to pop away from his barrel chest.

"Was that Yuki Kanai from the third year class?" asked Mister Sakata. "I didn't know you two knew each other. What were you talking about, Sawako?"

"Nothing." She wouldn't look him in the eyes. Mister Sakata liked to call the students by their first names. He probably did it to make them feel like he was their friend, but it made Sawako uncomfortable. She didn't want to get friendly with other people, especially teachers who thought they understood teenagers. But his searching gaze made her squirm. "What do you want?"

"I just wanted to ask you something."

What is this, Interrogate Sawako Day? "What?"

"It's about last Friday. I was out that day, so I didn't realize until I checked the attendance logs, but they say you were absent that morning, but you were back in the afternoon."

"Yes . . ."

"But Miyako and Megumi told me they saw you coming to school in the morning."

Sawako was startled. What was with everyone keeping tabs on her all of a sudden?

After noting her reaction, Mister Sakata continued, "I don't know if you know this, but when you use your student card to log in at the computer room, it records when you were there. So I know that you came to school on Friday, but you spent the morning in the computer room instead of going to class."

Sawako's hands clenched into fists.

"I'm not mad at you, Sawako," said Mister Sakata in that awful, sympathetic-adult voice. "Did something bad happen to you? Is someone picking on you? Is it that Yuki Kanai?"

Sawako couldn't answer.

"I'm worried about you. Ever since you came here, you haven't really gotten along with the other kids. Would you like to talk to me about it?"

Mister Sakata put his hand on her shoulder.

"It's nothing!" She glared at him until he removed his hand. Then, as if that had released her, she ran off down the street.

"Hey, Sawako! Wait!"

She shook her head, trying to shake his voice from her ears, and kept running.

MAYUMI

MONDAY, OCTOBER 6, 5:47 PM.

NIHON JOSHI ACADEMY GYMNASIUM.

It was like a sauna inside the gym.

The enormous Nihon Joshi gym contained six badminton courts. But all the courts were full, with over sixty players, both high school juniors and seniors, training fanatically under the watchful eyes of their coaches.

Even for amateurs, badminton takes a lot of energy. But the Nihon Joshi players were all at the national level. The heat they generated clouded the windows, and their sweat pooled on the floor.

Mayumi dashed around the gym, mopping up the sweat before the players could slip in it. She carried an armload of towels and washcloths, and tubes full of shuttlecocks—everything but a racket.

"Mayumi, hand me that rag."

"Mayumi, we need a new shuttlecock!"

Before one person had finished calling for her help, another one needed her somewhere else. The squeaking of the players' shoes, the yells of triumph and command, and the smack of rackets against shuttlecocks echoed around the high ceilings.

Mayumi couldn't run across the courts and interrupt the games, so she ran along the edges and turned at right angles. Being a manager was quite a workout.

But Mayumi didn't mind, and not only because she was near her beloved Sayuri. As she skidded around the edge of Court 3, the cell phone in her pocket slapped against her side. The reminder of its tiny weight made her feel lighter.

"Aren't we low on washcloths?" asked Nagano. The *senpai,* or senior student, was the manager of the high school group, and was conferring with Sawada, the manager of the junior high school group. Nagano was a shadow captain. She always stood beside Coach Asano, and her job was to pass along his orders, check the equipment, and put together the practice schedules.

Mayumi ran up to the managers. "I'll get some for you."

Sawada looked surprised. "They're in the high school's Home Economics room. You don't know where that is, do you, Mayumi?"

"Sure I do. I sneak into the high school sometimes."

Nagano's eyes narrowed at her confession.

"Okay, then. We're counting on you," said Sawada cheerfully. "There should be about thirty washcloths in the closet."

Mayumi sprinted for the exit. But when she emerged into the crisp fall air, instead of going to the high school, she dashed behind the gym. The only thing between the back of the gym and the back of a high-rise apartment building was a fence and a narrow strip of pavement, so no one was likely to pass by and catch Mayumi slacking off.

She was dying to find out if anyone had written anything else. The story was proceeding at a rapid clip, but it was driving Mayumi crazy that her character hadn't been introduced yet.

That girl Mai had easily entered into the story, but that was because her character already knew Sawako Shinoda. Mayumi's character was different. A detective couldn't just show up. Whether her character was a police officer or a private eye, she could only make an appearance after a crime had occurred. But Mayumi figured that Tetsuro had gotten scary enough by now that it would make sense for Sawako Shinoda to contact the police.

The sun had set, but there was plenty of ambient light from windows and streetlights. Mayumi settled down on the ground and opened her cell phone.

DATE AND TIME: OCTOBER 6, 4:53 PM

AUTHOR: MAI

CHARACTER: KOUHEI KIMURA

I met Sawako at a Starbucks in Naka-Meguro. While I drank my black coffee and she sipped her chestnut latte, she told me her theory that Tsunoda had gone to her mother and gotten her to fire me. If her mother had fired me because she'd gotten suspicious for no good reason, I don't think I would have met with Sawako. In fact, between Sawako's flirting and her mother's paranoia, I might have quit eventually on my own accord. But this stalker thing made me worried that Sawako might be in real trouble.

It was bad enough that he waylaid Sawako and spied on her, but for him to go to her mother and get me fired, just because he thought I might be a rival, suggested a disturbing level of obsession.

And that he'd managed to ingratiate himself with Mrs. Shinoda meant that he was intelligent enough to come up with a convincing cover story.

"What he's been doing is definitely a crime," I said. It felt funny to talk to her aloud after we'd spent such a long time only communicating in writing. "You should go to the police and tell them this guy is stalking you."

Sawako's eyes went wide at my mention of the police. "I can't go to the police. What if they talk to my mother?"

"So what if they do? When people are being stalked and they just ignore it, it only makes the stalker think he needs to do more to get their attention. Sometimes the victims actually get murdered."

Sawako's cheeks paled. I hastily added that *most* stalkers never physically attack their victims.

"But do you think the police will believe me?" she asked.

"Sure they will. Anyway, I've seen him too, so I'll go with you. I wonder what precinct is ours?"

But even as I spoke so confidently, I began to worry. Maybe the police wouldn't believe her. I'd heard that stalking was a very difficult crime to prove. And if Tsunoda found out that Sawako had gone to the police and the police blew her off, that would only encourage him.

I remembered a news story a while back. A woman had been stalked and the police ignored her reports. The stalker took that as a good sign and escalated his pursuit. Eventually, he murdered her. I couldn't let that happen to her. Sawako *had* to get police protection.

"I've got it!" I exclaimed. Sawako was so startled at my sudden outburst that she spilled some of her latte on the table. "One of my classmates from the tennis club has an older sister who's a cop. We can go talk to her. Her brother can vouch for me, and I'll vouch for you."

Sawako didn't seem as happy as I would have expected. "Is this classmate a woman?"

I was confused at first, but then I realized that she still suspected that I had something going on with the girl I'd been with at the tournament. "No, it's a guy. And I'll call him right now."

I took out my cell phone.

"All right!" Mayumi jumped to her feet and struck a victory pose like Sayuri did when one of her smashes got through.

Her turn had finally come. She wondered if Mai was deliberately giving her a chance to get in or if she was just going with the flow of the story.

But it didn't matter. It was finally the detective's turn. And she'd better hurry, because the story wouldn't be able to proceed much further until the detective showed up.

DATE AND TIME: OCTOBER 6, 6:25 PM
AUTHOR: MAYUMI
CHARACTER: DETECTIVE MURATA

The setting sun glinted off the fountain at Suntory Hall, burning my eyes. I was five minutes late.

I had gotten off at the wrong subway stop. Sure, it wasn't my turf, but that was no excuse. Suntory Hall is a pretty well-known building.

Of course, I've never had any reason to see it for myself. I'm not into classical music. Hell, I'm not much into music in general. My favorite fictional detective, Harry Bosch, is a big fan of jazz, but that's because he works the Hollywood beat. There's not many jazz clubs in my precinct, Kodaira. There's plenty of J-rock and folk music, but that's for teenyboppers.

The pavilion was crowded with high-class middle-aged people, decked out in all the fancy gear this month's magazines had told them to buy.

My mind wandered back to Sawako's story. If a sleaze like the guy she'd described mixed with this crowd, he'd stand out like a toad in a ballroom. Most stalkers didn't like to draw attention to themselves, and preferred to catch their victims when no one else was around. Now the meetings at Meguro Bridge, that sounded more plausible.

Then I stopped wondering. He was there.

He stood by the ticket booth, looking exactly like Sawako and her college boy had described: a lanky guy with long greasy hair, wearing grubby jeans, with a pair of binoculars hanging around his neck. When I got closer, I could even see the pitted lenses of his glasses.

I stepped right up to him. I'm tall for a Japanese woman (5'8") and I like to use my height to intimidate people. I made sure I'd be looming over him when he turned around, and then I barked, "Mister Tsunoda?!"

He looked up at me in surprise, but didn't answer.

"I'm Sawako Shinoda's aunt."

Yes, this is illegal. Sue me. The laws on stalking are a lot less stringent than they ought to be and Tsunoda hadn't yet crossed the line into committing a crime. I had no ground to arrest him, and without that, flashing my badge would only enrage him—rage that he'd take out on Sawako.

Also, it amused me to think that if I did arrest him later and he complained that I'd posed as Sawako's aunt, the other cops would just laugh.

"It was very sweet of you to invite my niece to a concert," I said, letting the sarcasm show. "But she's not coming."

Tsunoda stared at me blankly through his thick lenses. Hoping to notch up the intimidation factor, I deliberately stood so that the sun would shine directly in his eyes, but that didn't seem to bother him.

"Sawako's not going to be able to meet you any more," I went on. "She's not yet sixteen and that's too young to date a fine young man like you."

"Is that what Sawako said?" His voice was higher than I had expected and sounded depressed rather than angry. His face was totally expressionless.

I decided to drop the sarcasm, since it didn't seem to be registering. "You can think that if you like."

He was silent. His glasses gleamed red as the sunset deepened. For the first time, I got a sense of why this guy had scared both Sawako and Kouhei, aside from his obviously obsessive behavior. I see a lot of freaks and perverts on the job, but Tsunoda was a special kind of creep. He seemed surrounded by cold air. It was hard to breathe around him and I was sorry that I'd started out standing so close.

Without saying anything, Tsunoda turned and walked away.

I guess I should have followed him. But he hadn't done anything illegal yet, and he was probably watching to see if I would tail him, so . . .

Who am I fooling? I didn't follow him because I didn't want to spend any more time in his presence. When he left, I was as relieved as if he'd been holding me at gunpoint, and now I was free.

When Mayumi returned to the gymnasium, she was dismayed to see Nagano waiting for her in front of the entrance.

"Where have you been?" Nagano demanded.

"I'm sorry," said Mayumi. "The Home Ec room was locked, so I had to go look for someone with a key, and—"

Nagano cut her off. "Sawada and I got worried about you, so we went to the room. It wasn't locked. And you weren't there."

Oops.

It hadn't occurred to Mayumi that anyone would go looking for her. Then again, she'd only meant to write for ten minutes, not thirty.

Sawada came up to join Nagano. "Where have you been?" asked Sawada, in the exact same disapproving tone Nagano had used a moment earlier.

"My mother called." It was the only thing Mayumi could think of off-hand.

"Called?" echoed Nagano. "You're not telling me you brought your cell phone, are you?" Nagano's sharp gaze swept over Mayumi's body, then stopped at the rectangular bulge in her jersey pocket. "I can't believe you'd break the rules like that. You know what would happen if the coach found out?"

Sawada picked up where Nagano had left off. "Coach Nakazawa already thinks you've been up to something—he's the one who sent us to look for you."

Mayumi gritted her teeth. The junior high badminton team had two coaches. The woman, Coach Asano, was tough but approachable, and was always willing to explain the purpose of her drills. Coach Nakazawa was older, in his mid-forties, and never explained anything. He never spoke when he could shout, and handed out push-ups at the slightest infraction. None of the students liked him, and none of them would go up against him.

Nagano softened at Mayumi's silent misery. "I'll tell Coach Nakazawa that your mother sent a message to you."

Mayumi bowed to Nagano. "Thank you."

"But don't take off again, okay? I hate to say it, but Coach Nakazawa doesn't like you. I mean, even more than he doesn't like most people."

"I know," said Mayumi glumly. She'd heard through the grapevine that Coach Asano had been the one who had pushed through Mayumi's acceptance into the school—despite Coach Nakazawa's objections. Apparently the two coaches had never gotten along and their rift had widened over the fight they'd had about Mayumi's presence on the team.

"All right, then," said Nagano. She and Sawada turned to go back inside.

"Thank you!" called Mayumi, bowing to the door as it closed behind them. But her mind was already elsewhere.

I wonder if Detective Murata would carry a gun.

MAI
WEDNESDAY, OCTOBER 8, 8:07 AM.
YOTSUYA, SUBDIVISION 3, MAI'S HOUSE.

"Goodbye!" Mai put her hand on the front door.

"Mai, wait!" called her mother.

"What?" asked Mai. "I have to get to school."

"This'll only take a minute. It's about your tutor."

Mai was taken aback. The only tutor she was connected with was Kouhei Kimura. Had her mother found the *Chain Mail* site?

"The head of the Parent's Association called yesterday. You know, the Kabuki actor's wife."

Mai let out the breath she'd been holding. The Kabuki actor and his wife were the parents of one of her classmates, so this must have something to do with Mai's school, not her online life.

There's now way Mom would ever find out about that. She hardly even uses the home computer.

Her mother, typically, hadn't noticed Mai's moment of alarm, and had talked right through it. "And while her husband was doing the Kabuki show in New York, your father did a lot to help advertise it. They're good friends, you know."

"Mom, I'm going to be late."

"Sorry, I'll talk faster," her mother said blithely. "Anyway, their son has a tutor, and they asked if we'd like to have him coach you too.

He's a law student at Tokyo University, and they say he's a very good teacher."

"I don't need a tutor. My school's attached to Shirogane University, so as long as I keep getting the grades I'm getting now, I'll be accepted for sure."

"Don't be overconfident," her mother warned. "They waived the entrance exam for you because you were coming back from living overseas. But Shirogane Preparatory High School is one of the highest ranked girls' schools in Japan. Most of the other girls had to pass an exam to get in. So you'll have to beat some tough competition to get into Shirogane University's law school."

"I'm not applying to law school."

Mai's mother's stared at her daughter in astonishment. "Don't say that. Your father's looking forward to you going to law school, then joining him at the Ministry of Foreign Affairs."

Mai's chest filled with a rush of heat, as if someone had lit a match in her heart. "You can't decide that for me! It's *my* life."

Her mother fell silent before the force of Mai's anger.

"You and Dad can't keep running my life without ever asking me how I feel about it. I had a lot of friends here in Tokyo, but you decided to move us all to New York City because 'it would help my English.' Then when I finally started making friends in New York, you decided, 'if we go back now, Shirogane Preparatory will let her in automatically as a student returning from abroad.' Did you ever think I might have some feelings about any of that?"

"It was all for your own good," protested her mother.

"What do you mean, 'for my own good'?!" shouted Mai. "That's not *your* decision to make. *I'm* the only one who knows what's right for me!"

Mai grabbed her bag and ran out the front door. She slammed it behind her, cutting off the sound of her mother calling her name. She stomped past a quiet temple, ignoring the brilliant yellow ginkgo leaves that fluttered down around her.

Stupid tutor. As if they don't control enough of my time already. Kabuki actor . . . Ministry of Foreign Affairs . . . Shirogane University Law School . . . Who cares?!

She pretends to be such a with-it, understanding mother, but where is she when it really counts? She talks about letting me be my own person and making my own decisions, but when it comes to action, she's just as controlling as all the other mothers.

Mai passed a bank of vending machines, three selling coffee and tea, two selling soft drinks, and one selling beer. She fed in some coins and bought a can of hot Suntory Boss coffee with cream and sugar, and held it in both hands to savor the warmth as she sipped and walked. Then she turned a corner and came to a radio station. A group of girls her age were clustered around the entrance, probably waiting for some musician who was going to appear on a show.

Stupid groupies. Do they really think any musician is going to be happy to see anyone this early in the morning? Young people, old people, high schoolers, parents—at that moment, Mai despised the entire world. Luckily, there was another one. She took out her cell phone.

```
DATE AND TIME: OCTOBER 6, 10:03 PM
AUTHOR: YUKARI
CHARACTER: TETSURO TSUNODA
    That woman is a cop.
    I knew it the moment I looked into her eyes. It doesn't
matter how they act or how they're dressed. You can always
tell a cop by their suspicious eyes-the way they squint as
they try to see through your lies. That woman had the look
of a man-hunter.
    I never thought Sawako would call the police. That Kimura
guy must have talked her into it. Still, Sawako needs to
take responsibility for making the call.
    Why does she hate me? I think about her all the time.
Everything I do, I do for her. So why did she sic that cop
on me? I don't deserve to be hunted like a criminal.
    I have to make Sawako drop this crazy scheme. I have to
show her what a good person I am.
```

DATE AND TIME: OCTOBER 7, 3:05 AM
AUTHOR: SAWAKO
CHARACTER: SAWAKO SHINODA

"Kouhei, I'm scared." I clutched the phone, wishing it was Kouhei's hand. "It was in my mailbox when I got home."

I was afraid to look at the thing on the floor, but I was afraid to turn my back on it, too. It was a big teddy bear, like the one I had on my bed. But this one's stomach had been ripped open and stuffing was spilling out of the jagged slash. A paring knife was embedded deep in the middle of the wound.

"Have you told your mother?" Kouhei's voice sounded tinny, and I had to strain to hear him over the street noise in the background.

"She's on an overnight trip with the neighborhood block association. And my father always comes home late. I'm going to be alone 'til midnight."

It bothered me to see the knife impaling the teddy bear, so I pulled it out. It was so sharp that its edge sliced a new gouge into the bear's side, even though I hadn't pulled hard.

"Kouhei, I'm really scared. Please come over, right now!"

"I can't." He sounded frustrated. "I'm at tennis camp, all the way in Yamanashi prefecture. We're not due back until the day after tomorrow. But I'll call Detective Murata as soon as I hang up. In the meantime, make sure the house is locked up tight. And no matter what happens, don't go outside."

As soon as I hung up, I ran from window to window, closing all the rain shutters. I started with the first floor, then moved upstairs. The last window was the one over my desk in my room on the second floor. The curtains were already drawn. I stood there for a while, afraid to go any closer. To reach the rain shutters, I'd have to open the curtains.

Reluctantly, I pushed the light cloth aside. The sun had set, and there weren't many streetlights on my block. It was hard to see anything but shadows. But I didn't hear any suspicious noises, and it didn't look like anyone was down there. Relieved, I reached for the rain shutter.

A car drove by and its headlights momentarily illuminated the street below. As it passed a telephone pole, a flash of light pierced the shadows.

I stared hard at the place where the gleam of light had been. As my eyes grew accustomed to the darkness, I saw what had caused it. The headlights had reflected off of two glass lenses.

Tsunoda stood at the telephone pole. He was watching me through his binoculars.

```
DATE AND TIME: OCTOBER 7, 1:04 PM
AUTHOR: YUKARI
CHARACTER: TETSURO TSUNODA
```

Sawako won't come out of her house. She got the gift that I sent, but I'm not sure she understood its message.

The knife symbolizes the pure soul. (In Japanese tales, the God Susano-O slew an eight-headed serpent, and inside the beast's tail he found the sword called Grasscutter. In British legend, the boy Arthur is acknowledged as the rightful king when he pulls Excalibur out of a stone.) The sharp edge and shining blade represent the righteous person who cuts away all that is impure and evil.

As mothers sometimes have to be cut open to release their child, the wounded belly of the bear represents the birth of a new life. It's the birth of Sawako and me. The birth of a sacred couple.

Sawako is the perfect union of beauty and intelligence. Is it possible that someone as smart as her wouldn't understand this?

No. It's not possible.

She understands. She just doesn't know how to reply. Sawako is still very young. This filthy world hasn't taught her how to accept a holy gift.

That's why I have to take the next step.

I am a good person. I will show Sawako the way.

DATE AND TIME: OCTOBER 7, 10:03 PM
AUTHOR: MAYUMI
CHARACTER: DETECTIVE MURATA

Kouhei called me last night and told me about the teddy bear. When a man sends a woman a stuffed animal, he's sending her the message that he wants to hold her like she'd hold it. When he sends her a bear slashed open with a knife sticking out of it, he's telling her that he'll do the same to her unless she does exactly what he wants. But I had no intention of letting the matter progress any further than it already had.

I'm in charge of six police officers in my department. I had Officer Nakagawa look up Tetsuro Tsunoda. We have a database that allows us to look up anyone who's ever been charged with a crime in Japan. If Tsunoda had a prior record, and I bet he did, I'd know it in a second.

I went to the staff room and got a cold can of black coffee from the vending machine. When I came back, Nakagawa beckoned me. "Detective Murata, I've got the goods on that Tsunoda guy."

There was a mug shot of Tsunoda on his computer screen, and the following details below: *Tetsuro Tsunoda. Age twenty-two. Resides in Himonya, Meguro Ward, Tokyo.*

I nodded. That's Sawako's neighborhood.

Nakagawa summarized the charges. "Last year he stalked a high school girl and broke into her house. It was his first offense, so he got a suspended sentence."

"Once a stalker, always a stalker," I snarled, scribbling down his address.

"Detective Murata, is this guy involved in a case of yours?"

"Might be," I said. "Anyway, thanks." I patted Nakagawa on the shoulder and left the office.

Since Tsunoda and Sawako were both in Himonya, this case came under the jurisdiction of the Himonya precinct. I thought of contacting them, but the superintendent there was a real old-guard type, the sort who dismissed stalking victims as sufferers of schoolgirl hysteria—and it didn't help that the victim actually was a schoolgirl. In any case, it would be hard to prove that Tsunoda had sent the teddy bear, or, without a note attached, that he meant it as a death threat.

I had other reasons for wanting to keep this case to myself. Most of the crime I deal with is minor: burglaries where no one gets hurt, or assaults where the victim's injuries are no worse than they'd get if they took a spill on their bicycle. But when I looked into Tsunoda's eyes, I sensed an endless darkness unfolding within him. I've been a cop for a long time, and he set off all my alarm bells. I had a feeling that he had more potential for horrifying violence than anyone I'd ever met.

I wanted to go after him myself. I set out right away.

Tsunoda's home was a ten-minute walk from Gakugei University station on the Toyoko train line. It was a first floor apartment in a two-story wooden building. A rusted mailbox bore the sloppy inscription, "Tsunoda."

I knocked on the thin vinyl door. The dry sound echoed and died. There was no response. I tried the doorknob, but it was locked.

"Nobody home, huh?" I asked loudly.

I considered going to Sawako's house, but it was a weekday and she'd be in school. Instead, I started knocking on doors, asking the neighbors about Tsunoda while I waited for him to come home.

DATE AND TIME: OCTOBER 8, 12:07 AM
AUTHOR: SAWAKO
CHARACTER: SAWAKO SHINODA

I stayed home from school today. I was too scared to leave the house.

I didn't tell my father about Tsunoda, since he'd reacted so badly when I'd tried to tell him that someone was watching me. He'd looked at me like *I* was the one who had done something wrong. If I told him now, he'd give me that same awful look, half-disgusted and half-scared, and then watch me to make sure I went to school.

I wish Kouhei was here. But he wouldn't be back from his training camp until tomorrow. I have to protect myself until then. Just thinking that makes me want to crawl into bed and pull the covers over my head.

I paced around the living room and dining room, frantic with worry. After a while, I realized that I was standing in front of the refrigerator. Without thinking about it or noticing what I'd been doing, I had opened it and was rummaging through the pickled vegetables and leftover noodles, looking for something to eat. Even when I was terrified for my life, I still got hungry and went looking for a snack.

I hated the way an instinct like hunger could override my conscious mind. If God had created us, why had he saddled us with emotions and instincts? Was it to make us suffer? A person whose house had burned down will sit down in the ashes and cry. But a few hours later, he'll sit again in those same ashes and eat. And when he realizes what he's doing, it'll make him so sad that he'll cry again.

The doorbell rang. I froze with a rice ball half-way to my mouth.

It rang again.

I assured myself that it couldn't be Tsunoda. He always stood in the shadow of the telephone pole and watched me through my window. He had never once walked through the front gate and up to the door in broad daylight.

But if it wasn't Tsunoda, then who was it?

And what if it was Tsunoda? He might have gotten tired of waiting, especially now that he can't see inside.

I had to check. I put the rice ball down on the counter, then tiptoed to the bathroom and gently pulled the door open. The floor creaked wherever I walked. But I took a deep breath, then stepped up onto the lid of the toilet seat. From that vantage point, I could stand on the balls of my feet and peek out of the bathroom's high window to the front of the house.

A man in a gray shirt and pants stood in front of the door. He had a gray hat pulled down to shade his eyes, and a nametag on his shirt. He held a clipboard, and there was a package at his feet.

Oh, it's a deliveryman.

The doorbell rang for the third time.

"Coming!" I yelled.

"I've got a package for a Miss Shinoda!" called the deliveryman. "It needs her signature."

"I'll be right there!" I searched for a pen, found it in my desk drawer, then ran to the foyer. I undid the chain lock, the deadbolt, and the doorknob lock, then opened the door.

"Here's your package," mumbled the deliveryman, looking at the ground. His hat was pulled down so far over his face that I was surprised he could see anything.

He held the clipboard while I signed. There was a bandage wrapped around his pinky, but it didn't seem to bother him when he handed the package to me. Our fingers brushed as I took it, and I felt a shudder go through his body.

The package was big, but very light. It was addressed to me in handwriting I didn't recognize. The return address was for the "Fall Gift Campaign Office." I had no idea what it could be.

The deliveryman bowed. "Thank you very much." He closed the steel gate behind him with a clink.

I locked the door, then began to open the package. I had to tug hard to get the packing tape off, and as I did that I could hear something rattle gently, like postcards in a half-empty box of stationery.

As I pried up the last strip of tape, something occurred to me. Where had the deliveryman parked his truck?

Whenever deliverymen come by, I always hear their trucks pulling up in front of the house. Then I hear the engine turning off, the door closing after the driver gets out, and the back of the truck being opened and closed. Only then does the doorbell ring. When they leave, it goes in reverse. The driver closes the door after he gets inside, the engine starts, and its noise fades into the distance. It wasn't something I'd thought much about, but I noticed when it didn't happen this time.

The man had just appeared, and then he'd left without a sound. But a deliveryman had to have a vehicle.

It couldn't have been . . .

The cardboard box on the floor suddenly seemed ominous. I was almost afraid to touch the last piece of tape. I finally yanked it off as fast as I could, as if I was ripping off a band-aid.

The box contained an envelope. Nothing more.

I opened it. There was a piece of folded notepaper inside. When I pulled out the paper, two tickets fell out of the envelope and fluttered to the floor. I stooped and picked them up.

The tickets were for the bullet train: *October 11, 10:56 AM. Kodama train 413, from Tokyo to Mishima. Seats 12 D and E in car 12.*

I unfolded the note. It was written in wet, red letters.

Dear Sawako~

If you are reading this letter, then my fingers touched yours. That's proof that we are bound together.

You probably noticed that my finger was bandaged.

For you, I shed my blood.

For you, I show the proof of my love.

Now, bride of the blood, it is your turn to prove yourself.

You will go on a trip with me. We will go to the promised land together.

I don't need to tell you what will happen if you reject me.

~From a good person.

My vision started to blur. My legs felt weak, so I put a hand to the wall to steady myself.

The letter fell to the floor, faster than the tickets had because it was wet and weighted with blood.

It landed on my feet. I felt his blood touch my skin. The red letters clung to my flesh as if they were embracing me.

Then everything went black.

Mai closed her cell phone with a sigh of satisfaction. She'd been so engrossed in the story that she had almost missed her stop at Shinjuku, where she had to change trains.

The other writers are so talented, she thought wistfully. Her awkward Kouhei couldn't measure up to Sawako's terrified Sawako Shinoda, Mayumi's hard-bitten Detective Murata, or Yukari's psychopathic Tsunoda. Mai felt as if she was a junior high student who'd blundered into a college class, trying hopelessly to keep up with students who'd been studying the material for years.

Sawako's latest entries had sent Kouhei away to Yamakakako, so he couldn't get back into the story right away. Mai was grateful for the excuse to put off writing his story. But he would have to come back soon, and she had no idea what to do with him.

It wasn't just that she was insecure about her writing ability. Mai couldn't imagine sweet, tennis-playing Kouhei Kimura going up against the insane stalker Yukari had created. When Mai had read the bit about "bride of the blood," she'd involuntarily looked around in the crowded train to make sure that a young man with smeary glasses and a bandaged finger wasn't standing right behind her. How had Yukari come up with a character like that? It was hard to believe that he was fictional. Kouhei was only a character Mai had imagined, but Tsunoda seemed real.

And so did Sawako. Mai couldn't help worrying for her. It was silly, but Mai felt like there really was a girl named Sawako who really was in danger.

She wondered how the story would end. It unnerved her that there was no way to find out until it happened. If *Chain Mail* was a published novel, she'd skip to the last page now. It would be worth sacrificing the pleasure of suspense to know for sure that there'd be a happy ending, or to be able to brace herself should there be a sad one.

But *Chain Mail* wasn't a book, or at least not a published one. The ending had not been written. No one knew what would happen next, or if the end would be tragic. Just like the real world.

It was raining when Mai left Gotanda station. She opened her umbrella, but the rain blew sideways and dripped down her ankles and soaked her feet.

Bride of the blood, she thought, and shivered.

SAWAKO

THURSDAY, OCTOBER 9, 4:13 PM.

SHIBUYA STATION, LOCAL STOP TOYOKO LINE.

Sawako walked up the stairs of Shibuya station to catch the slowest train on the Toyoko line. Commuters hurried past her like busy ants.

It would have been more convenient, not to mention faster, if she'd been willing to take the limited express. But she never caught those trains. It wasn't because they were more crowded than the local stops or because she hated standing. She just didn't like their atmosphere.

She had started taking the train to school when she joined Kioi Academy. That was when she'd noticed that the air inside the local stop trains was different from that in the express trains. Express train air hummed with the desire to get home fast, or get to work fast, or go to some favorite place to slack off fast. Those trains were suffused with think positive, work hard-play hard, go-go-go vibrations.

But the air currents in the local stop trains whispered, "It doesn't matter what happens." They murmured, "Relax." Sawako was especially fond of the sleepy feeling of the Toyoko local stop train, as it leisurely crossed the steel bridge at Tamagawa.

Not everyone who rode the express trains was energetic. If you looked around Shibuya station, you'd see plenty of tired businessmen dragging their heavy bodies to the express trains and beaching themselves on the seats like whales. If you stuck a microphone in their faces and demanded an answer for the record, they might say, "To be honest, I'd rather take my time and catch a local train. But I have to get to work early. It's not up to me."

But Sawako thought that a person who'd say that couldn't hate their job. If they really couldn't stand it, they'd have already quit and ride the local.

Just like her mother.

Sawako's mother had hated her father. That's why she quit. She left everything behind and started living a laid-back life, riding the local.

That's why Sawako always took it too.

It wasn't quite rush hour, and her train was almost empty. Across the platform, people crammed themselves into a limited express. All its seats were full, and an assortment of businessmen, schoolgirls, office ladies, old men, old ladies in kimono, and cosplaying teenagers in Gothic Lolita outfits stood by the doors. But there was only one other person in Sawako's car. If anyone had wanted to, they could have stretched out full-length on the seven-person bench, and let the sound of the rails lull them to sleep.

Each car on the Toyoko line had a few four-person box seats, like the ones on the long-distance trains. But most people didn't use them, except during rush hours when those were the only seats left. The seats were too close together, so people's knees touched, and a person with long legs would be miserable. Needless to say, if you didn't have a book or cell phone to look at, you either had to stare directly at a stranger or consciously avert your eyes. And since the box seats were so unpopular, sitting in one guaranteed her privacy.

Sawako took out her cell phone. She was happy with the way *Chain Mail* was going. Everyone was good at sustaining the excitement. Mayumi seemed to know an uncanny amount about how a policewoman would think. Mai didn't seem as accomplished a writer as the others, but her Kouhei did seem like someone Sawako Shinoda would be attracted to and trust with her secrets.

But the best one was Yukari. Her stalker was genuinely scary. Even though Sawako knew it was just a story, she sometimes wondered if someone might be watching her through binoculars. Maybe it hadn't been such a great idea to name her character after herself.

Tsunoda was quickly escalating the level of obsession and violence. When Sawako imagined what might happen if he and Sawako Shinoda were real people, it made her feel weak in the knees.

Chain Mail popped up on the screen. There were two new entries.

DATE AND TIME: OCTOBER 9, 12:47 PM

AUTHOR: MAI

CHARACTER: KOUHEI KIMURA

I couldn't stop staring at the blood-smeared letter.

Sawako had told me what had happened over the phone, but that was different from seeing it in person. The words on the page were rusty brown, like a stained bandage tossed in the trash. I didn't want to touch it.

"This can't be legal," I said. "Tsunoda should be arrested."

Sawako was silent. She was staring up at the ceiling. I guess she didn't want to look at me because I was standing by the kitchen table, which was where the letter was. The mutilated teddy bear was there too, and the paring knife beside it. We had set them out as evidence to hand over to Detective Murata. Sawako didn't want to have anything more to do with them, even though we really needed them to prove Tsunoda's guilt.

I could understand. I didn't like to look at them either. Still, I was the one who fished them out of the trashcan and carried them to the kitchen.

Detective Murata was late. When I'd called her, she'd said she'd come over immediately. I guess it's a long way from the Kodaira precinct to Sawako's house in Setagaya.

"You've got to tell your parents what's going on," I said.

Sawako wouldn't look at me. Eventually, she shook her head.

"Once your mother comes back from her trip, I won't be able to stay here with you."

At that, Sawako met my eyes, her gaze glinting with held-in tears. "Don't leave me, Kouhei."

"I won't, for now. And I'll come with you when you go out."

Sawako just sniffled.

"If you're having a hard time talking to your father, I'll tell him for you." I took out my cell phone. "What's his number?"

"It won't help!" blurted out Sawako. "You can't tell my mother, either!"

"But, Sawako . . ."

"Don't you understand? They'll blame *me!*"

I was shocked that she would think that of her own parents. "But you're the victim."

She laughed bitterly. "My father will say, 'This would never have happened if you hadn't spoken to strangers.' He'll assume I flirted with Tsunoda and led him on." The tears in her right eye spilled over and ran down her cheek. "And my mother—she'll be furious with me for calling the police. She'll say, 'Everything the police know, the press knows. What's going to happen to your father when this hits the papers? A scandal could ruin his career.' "

I had forgotten that Sawako's father worked for the Ministry of Foreign Affairs. Sawako never discussed it with me, but the first day

I'd come in to tutor her, her mother proudly informed me that her husband had graduated from Tokyo University and was a high-ranking diplomat.

"It doesn't matter who your parents are," I told Sawako. "All they'll care about is that their daughter's in danger."

"You don't understand what kind of people they are!" Sawako shouted. "My uncle owns a restaurant. Last year it went under. You know what the first thing they said to him was? 'You didn't try to keep it afloat by borrowing any money from gangsters, did you? If you get involved in a scandal, it'll ruin us all!' They only started consoling him after he promised that he hadn't done anything shady."

There was nothing I could say. I knew she wasn't lying, so I had to believe that some people *were* like that. But it was weird to have a junior high school girl teach me to see the world without rose-tinted glasses.

Was it a mistake to contact Detective Murata? When Mrs. Shinoda found out that a detective had come to her house, will she be outraged? Will Sawako's parents really not care that their daughter's life was in danger?

I stood silently in the kitchen with a sobbing girl, a ruined toy, a bloody note, and a very sharp knife . . . and no idea what would happen next.

Sawako smiled as she closed Mai's entry. *She hates her parents,* thought Sawako. She was positive that Mai hadn't put in all that stuff about Sawako Shinoda's unsympathetic parents merely to raise the stakes. Her other entries had also had a lot of anger directed at the heroine's parents: her mother had spied on her and then fired her tutor, and her father always worked late and rarely came home.

It might be that Mai wasn't used to writing fiction. Since she'd joined *Chain Mail*, she probably liked to read, but maybe she'd never written anything before other than e-mails to her friends. Since she wasn't used to making up stories, she might have automatically described her real family in order to flesh out Sawako Shinoda's background.

Or maybe she was so self-absorbed that her own life was the only reality she could imagine.

Neither of those possibilities bothered Sawako. She understood Mai's problem. No matter how hard you try to create a story that's completely fictional, parts of your own experience are bound to surface.

Anyway, it might be fun to add a little more reality to the fictional world. The most gripping stories were the ones that seemed closest to real life. What better way to make *Chain Mail* more realistic than to add some real-life elements to it?

Maybe I'll try that too, thought Sawako. *I'll have Mister Shinoda blame his daughter for attracting a stalker's attention. I know just what he can say to make the readers hate him.*

He can say, "It's your mother's fault. It's her bad genes coming out!" That will make him the perfect villain.

Sawako suddenly turned her head. She had the feeling that someone was watching her.

The train had just left Metropolitan University station without picking up any more passengers. The only other people in the car were a businessman in a navy blue suit, a mother with a baby carriage, a boy with a red baseball cap turned backward, and a high school girl who wasn't wearing a uniform.

The businessman was asleep, the girl and mother were looking at their cell phones, and the boy was reading a manga about ninja fighting giant squid, if the page it was open to was representative. None of them were watching Sawako.

It must have been my imagination.

She returned to *Chain Mail*. But she couldn't focus. *It was because I thought about Dad.* Understanding the source of her anxiety banished it. She brushed the image of her father's face from her mind, and opened the next entry.

```
DATE AND TIME: OCTOBER 9, 2:17 PM
AUTHOR: YUKARI
CHARACTER: TETSURO TSUNODA
```

That female detective was in Sawako's house. How could Sawako have allowed her inside? I guess Sawako didn't accept my message.

She should have understood what I was feeling when I wrote to her. She should have appreciated how I dealt with the pain of my wound, and kept on writing. She should have responded to the call of my blood.

But she didn't. And now I have to deal with that woman detective. I never imagined that she would find my address so quickly, or that she would care enough to show up in my neighborhood and start inquiring about me. I underestimated her. But I won't make that mistake again.

That time when I was interested in that other girl, she told her parents about me, and they went straight to the police. But it took the cops two months just to figure out my name, and a month after that to catch me. So I figured all cops were morons.

But this woman detective found my address in a day. If I hadn't happened to be at the bank when she came to my house, and if my landlord hadn't tipped me off that she'd been asking about me, I might have walked right into her.

That bitch. I won't forget about this.

No, I shouldn't hate her. If I hate her, that's putting her on the same level as me—maybe even higher. We hate people who are more powerful than us. So, I despise her. I hold her in contempt. But I don't hate her.

Besides, she was the reason I got a blessing from God. It was God who sent me to the bank, and God who made my landlord tell me she was looking for me. These things don't happen by chance. I'm being protected. God is protecting me because I'm a good person. God would never allow a good person to become a victim. So I'll just keep going. With God on my side, I have nothing to worry about.

```
     I will achieve my goal. I will make Sawako my wife.
     I will also show that bitch detective and wimpy boyfriend
what an amazing person I am.
     To do all that, I have to watch Sawako. I can't stop
watching her, not even for a minute.
     Just as God is watching over me. God wants good people
to do good things.
     So I'll just keep watching over her. My chance to steal
her away will come.
```

Sawako shivered and rubbed the base of her neck. She still couldn't shake the feeling of being watched. It was probably just her imagination.

She slowly looked up.

There *was* someone watching her. It was a girl at the other end of the compartment. She was wearing a tank top, even though it was October. She held her cell phone up to her face, but her piercing gaze was aimed straight at Sawako.

Sawako didn't recognize her, and she'd have remembered if anyone had ever stared at her with eyes like those.

"We are now approaching Shin-Maruko," announced the conductor. "Next stop, Shin-Maruko."

It wasn't Sawako's stop, but she got up anyway. It was only a five-minute walk to the next station. And if that girl followed Sawako, then she'd know for sure that something strange was up.

But if there is something weird going on, what do I do?

The train slowed down. There was no time to strategize. Sawako was too nervous to stay on the same train as that girl, so she'd just leave.

The train stopped. The doors slid open. Sawako got up. As soon as she stood, so did the girl in the tank top. The two of them stepped on to the platform together. And when Sawako turned to glance at the girl, she saw that the boy in the red baseball cap had joined them.

The girl and boy were both after Sawako.

III.

"The surest way to corrupt a youth is to instruct him to hold those who think alike in higher esteem than those who think differently."

NIETZSCHE
THE DAWN

The old lady who ran the corner store smiled sympathetically as she packed a cardboard box with bottles of oolong tea. "This must be tough for you, Mayumi. You're still so young and your school makes you train so hard. I don't like the idea of you working hard during vacations. Your body needs time to recover. And you're such a little thing, too."

"It's all right," replied Mayumi. She pulled money out of an envelope marked "Nihon Joshi," and put it in the change tray. "Anyway, it's hard on everyone, not just me."

"You're so responsible," said the lady with a sigh. She counted out the change. "I wish you'd talk to my lazy son. Here, take this." She reached up to the shelf and handed Mayumi a can of hot green tea.

Mayumi bowed her head in thanks and popped the canned tea into her bag. But when she tried to lift the two cardboard boxes off the counter, she staggered. They each contained twelve one-liter bottles of tea, and were heavier than she had expected.

"We can deliver them for you," offered the old lady.

"No, no, I can do it," said Mayumi. "My bicycle is right over there, so. . ."

Mayumi wobbled left and right as she lugged the boxes out of the store, but she managed to not drop anything. She put them in the basket of her vehicle, which was not a bicycle but a tricycle, like old women used to ride around the neighborhood streets. The basket between the rear wheels was enormous and had "Nihon Joshi Badminton Club" written on it in slightly crooked letters.

It was a three-day weekend, which the badminton club was celebrating in typical fashion by holding a training camp to prepare for the upcoming Junior National Finals. In addition to Mayumi's usual duties, she had to buy food and drinks for the players and coaches, and tea and snacks for the players' parents who came to watch. Tonight there was a party for the coaches and school alumni, so Mayumi would have to make a trip to another store to stock up on party food.

The grocery store wasn't crowded, but it was sprinkled with shoppers who came out of the drizzle. They all seemed happy and relaxed, enjoying the weekend.

A group of junior high school students chatted in front of a cell phone store, parents took their children out for ramen and hamburgers, and a high school couple shared an umbrella. Mayumi wished she was with them—any of them—rather than pedaling her old-lady tricycle in the rain, with sweat trickling down her temples and her scratchy uniform chafing.

She decided to take the back roads rather than the main streets. It'd take longer, but she wasn't in the mood for dodging traffic. Once she left the main street behind, the number of people in sight quickly dwindled.

A playground came into view, and it occurred to her that since no one was around, no one would see her if she stopped to check *Chain Mail*. Although even if no one saw her, they might still notice if she was late. Ever since the senior students had caught her lying about visiting the Home Ec room, they'd been watching her like a pair of athletically-inclined hawks.

Oh, who cares if they do notice?

Mayumi was startled to find herself thinking differently. She was usually obsessed with being the perfect club manager. It ought to upset her terribly if the coaches or seniors were unhappy with her. Badminton was the most important thing in the world to her, so she used to dash to and from errands to minimize how much time she lost when she could be watching Sayuri play.

Of course badminton is still the main thing I care about, Mayumi assured herself. Sure, *Chain Mail* was interesting. True, she did look forward to it. But it wasn't as if it could replace badminton.

For six years, Mayumi had devoted herself to badminton and Sayuri, and paid no attention to anything else. The thought that she might be losing her focus alarmed her. But before she could obsess, she spotted a bench. It was under a tree, so the seat was still dry.

She eagerly sat down and opened her umbrella in case it started raining harder. Balancing her umbrella against her shoulder, she popped the tab of the green tea can, then flipped open her cell phone. In an instant, she was immersed in the world of *Chain Mail*.

DATE AND TIME: OCTOBER 9, 5:27 PM
AUTHOR: SAWAKO
CHARACTER: SAWAKO SHINODA

Someone's following me.

It's a man. I don't know who he is. I got off the train, and he got off with me. I left the station, and he was behind me.

I didn't realize it at first. I did feel as if I was being watched, but I thought I was imagining things. I didn't see Tsunoda.

I ended up getting off the train before my usual stop. This boy wearing a red baseball cap got off too. I guess everyone has to leave eventually. But he exited at the exact same time as me.

I left the station and started walking. When I got to the residential area, I turned right and left at random. But no matter where I went, that man was always half a block behind me. His baseball cap was pulled down over his eyes, so I couldn't see his face. Tsunoda did that to disguise himself, but this guy seemed different. I don't know how he was different, he just was.

I started to panic. Why was he following me? Was it Tsunoda? Or was it someone else? Could Tsunoda have convinced someone else to follow me for him? Could I have attracted two stalkers?

Then I realized that I was lost. I didn't know the neighborhood. I hadn't been keeping track of where I had turned. I had no idea where I could go to escape the man.

I was in an alley. The buildings were old. All the windows were dark. The streets were deserted. It was so quiet.

I was really scared. I didn't know what to do, so I kept walking.

Mayumi was disappointed. She had read this entry two nights ago, when it had been posted. Usually someone posted an entry every day, but no one had posted now for a day and a half.

Of course, Mayumi was one of the people who hadn't been writing. But that was because she had expected that Yukari would write an entry from Tsunoda's point of view, explaining what was going on in Sawako's post. Mayumi had thought she'd better wait for Yukari to at least *hint* whether the man in the baseball cap was Tsunoda, or one of Tsunoda's friends, or someone else entirely, before Mayumi wrote an entry from Detective Murata's point of view. But Yukari hadn't written anything. Mayumi wondered what was up.

She kicked the ground in frustration, scattering some muddy gravel. It had started raining harder while she reread the last entry, and though her umbrella had protected her head and cell phone, she was drenched from the waist down. The rain had gotten inside her sneakers, and they felt soggy and disgusting.

Mayumi scowled. *What's wrong with everybody? Why aren't they writing? Have they all gotten bored and given up? How dare they?*

She kept checking in even though she was in the middle of an intensive training camp, she kept on writing even though she had to steal away to do so, she kept going even under the spying eyes of her coaches and seniors . . .

Speaking of spying eyes, there was something odd about Sawako's last entry. She usually wrote in a more polished style, with metaphors and neat turns of phrase. But this entry was rough and repetitive, as if it had been written in a hurry. It read more like a real diary entry than like a chapter in a book.

It wasn't that Sawako's other entries were unrealistic, but . . . the others were realistic in the way that a good book creates the illusion of reality. This one, though less artful, felt not realistic—but *real.*

It sounded as if the person who wrote it really was terrified.

Maybe Sawako is experimenting with different styles. But why hasn't she written anything after that one?

"Maybe she's busy with school," muttered Mayumi to herself. "But come on! I'm busy too."

She glanced at her watch. She was late already, but if she didn't write something right now, maybe the others would decide that everyone else had dropped out, and that would be the end of *Chain Mail.* It was up to her to save it. Mayumi clicked on "compose."

MAI
SATURDAY, OCTOBER 11, 4:37 PM.
TOKYO-TOYOKO LINE: A LOCAL TRAIN TO SHIBUYA.

Mai had a problem. She had no idea what to wear to the concert tomorrow.

Last night she had been surfing the Internet when she saw an ad for a new clothing store in Jiyugaoka. It was a long train ride and not one of her usual haunts, but Mai decided to check it out. The clothes weren't quite cutting edge, but there were plenty of classic styles, and the prices were outrageously cheap.

So Mai caught the train to Jiyugaoka, and discovered that the ad hadn't lied. She found a pair of sleek black leather pants for eighty-five hundred yen*, a studded leather vest for ninety-nine hundred yen, and a pair of thigh-high boots with silver buckles for just seven thousand yen. The leather was real, and the prices were a steal.

Mai's allowance was only five thousand yen per month, but she also got five hundred yen per day to buy lunch. Ever since she'd returned to Tokyo, she'd eaten a hearty breakfast at home so she could skip lunch and save the five hundred. She also saved the money she'd gotten from her relatives for New Year's Day. So even though she went to concerts twice a month, she still had quite a bit of money saved.

She had allotted herself thirty thousand yen to spend today at Jiyugaoka, provided the clothes were really as good as advertised. Normally, that would be nowhere near enough to completely deck out in black leather, but at this store, Mai calculated, she could buy boots, pants, and a vest, and still have about five thousand yen left over.

But she hadn't bought anything.

She found plenty of things she liked, and some of them even fit. But when she piled all of them into her arms to take over to the register, she abruptly lost her desire to buy them.

As she imagined purchasing the clothes—opening her wallet, taking out a ten thousand yen note, handing it over, and so forth— the whole thing suddenly seemed tawdry and depressing.

It wasn't that she was reluctant to spend money, or that she thought she'd be wasting it. The problem was that it wasn't *her* money. It had belonged to her parents. It was money they'd given her for this sort of thing. When she realized that, she didn't want to use it any more.

---

* $1 equals approximately ¥115. Mai's allowance is about $44 a month.

Mai felt strange thinking that. It wasn't as if she could buy more freedom and responsibility from her parents if she held off on buying clothes. She wasn't even being more independent, because she was still eating their food, living in their house, and going to a school they paid for. The only person who would be affected if she didn't buy the clothes was her.

She remembered what the groupies in Takadanobaba had said to her: "Rich bitch junior high school brat. We had to work to get the money for the concert, but her parents just hand it over every time she goes whining to them for more."

Even then, Mai had known that they'd had a point. She just didn't know what she could do about it. But now she felt that she had to do *something*. Even if it was a tiny, futile act of resistance, like not spending money they'd already given her, she still had to resist.

When she started college, she could get a part-time job. Once she did that, she'd have her own money that she'd be comfortable spending on concerts and clothes. Until then, well, she'd keep skipping lunch so she could afford concerts, because music was as necessary as food to her. But that would be it. She had plenty of clothes already, so she could simply wear the ones she had.

It was only six months until she started high school. The thought didn't make all her problems fade away, but it did make her feel a bit better.

The girl sitting beside her opened her cell phone and began to text-message someone.

Mai hadn't checked *Chain Mail* that day. As she rummaged in her bag for her cell phone, she realized that she felt oddly reluctant to log on. There had been something about the latest entry that had bothered her.

The number of new entries had slowed down recently, but that wasn't surprising. Second term was busy for everyone. There were lots of school festivals and trips. If any of the other girls were in a club, they'd have more practice sessions and matches to prepare for end-of-year tournaments. Plus there was the three-day weekend. Lots of schools, including Mai's, had held midterms right before it, so their students could use the weekend for relaxing instead of studying—which was why Mai hadn't posted either.

What worried Mai was Yukari's silence. She would have expected a post from Tsunoda immediately after Sawako had left such a desperate entry, gloating over how cleverly he'd followed her. And Sawako's post had been strange.

Her previous entries had been wonderfully scary, like the slasher movies she's seen in New York, but this one was disturbing in a different way. All that earlier stuff about "bride of the blood" and mutilated teddy bears had made Mai want to cover her eyes and squeal. But Sawako's last entry, though it had lacked flashy details, had scared Mai as if she had been in a car that hit a patch of ice and started to skid. It read like an SOS from the real Sawako, as if something had gone terribly wrong in her real life, and the only way she could deal with it was to pretend it was fiction.

The *Chain Mail* site finished loading. There was one new entry.

DATE AND TIME: OCTOBER 11, 3:55 PM.
AUTHOR: MAYUMI
CHARACTER: DETECTIVE MURATA

Why hasn't Sawako contacted me?

I gave her my cell number when I could have fobbed her off with the station number. I made every effort to help her unofficially, so that she could prevent her parents from finding out that she was being stalked. But she hasn't contacted me by phone or e-mail—not even once.

Kouhei Kimura, who seemed so upset on her behalf, hasn't bothered to call either. What kind of man is he? He insisted that I look into this, and now he's fallen off the face of the earth.

I stuck my neck out on their behalf. This case should belong to another precinct, and I should have reported it to them immediately.

I could get in trouble for this. But I didn't get involved merely because Kouhei is my little brother's friend. It was because, unlike some people on the force, I take stalking seriously—and personally.

Not taking no for an answer, following a woman because she turned you down, and threatening her as a way of forcing her into your arms is the absolute lowest crime there is.

I don't mind spending my off-duty hours trying to help Sawako. But no news isn't good news when you've got a stalking case. I can't help Sawako if she won't tell me what's going on.

I'm starting to get worried. I'll e-mail her and tell her to reply immediately, just so I know she's all right.

Man, she's pissed off.

Mai realized that she had been holding the cell phone at arm's length, as if Mayumi—or Detective Murata—might actually reach out and hit her.

But she could understand why Mayumi was angry. *Chain Mail* was a collaborative story, and it only worked if they all pulled their weight. With only four writers, the story slowed down if even one of them slacked off. And if three of the four writers didn't post in two days, *Chain Mail* was dead in the water.

Sorry, Mayumi, she thought. *I'll post right now.*

Even if she only wrote a little bit, at least that would tell everyone that she hadn't abandoned *Chain Mail.*

DATE AND TIME: OCTOBER 11, 4:46 PM.

AUTHOR: MAI

CHARACTER: KOUHEI KIMURA

I picked up the phone. Detective Murata started yelling even before I could get the receiver up to my ear.

"What in the world are you doing?! You haven't contacted me in two days!"

"I—I'm sorry . . ."

"Never mind apologizing, just tell me what's up with Sawako. Is she okay?"

"That's the problem. I haven't heard from her in two days."

"What did you say?" Detective Murata's voice sounded strained.

"Whenever I call her cell phone, I get the message that it's in an area with no signal."

"Oh . . . That's not good," Murata muttered. "Go to Sawako's house. If she's not there, ask her parents if they know where she is."

"But I thought we were trying to keep this thing a secret. I don't want her to get in trouble."

"If she gets in trouble, that means she's alive," snapped Murata. "If she's de—if something's happened to her, then she won't be in trouble no matter what her parents think."

I swallowed passed the lump in my throat. "I see what you mean. I'll go right now."

Stuffing my phone back in my pocket, I ran out the door.

Mai checked it for spelling errors, then sent it off. She didn't think it was all that inspired, but at least now everyone would know she was still there. And because she'd sent Kouhei to Sawako's house, Sawako would have to write a scene where he arrived.

As long as nothing has happened to her.

The train pulled out of Daikanyama station. Mai watched as it slowly passed the neighborhood's signature modernist buildings, elegant geometries of steel and glass and pastel porcelain tiles. As the train picked up speed, the rain seemed to fall horizontally, and the landscape became blurred.

Though she tried to suppress it, uneasiness welled up in Mai and filled her heart like cold, dirty water.

MAYUMI

MONDAY, OCTOBER 13, 1:20 PM.

NIHON JOSHI ACADEMY GYMNASIUM.

The bus rang with laughter and overlapping conversations. The Nihon Joshi Junior High Badminton Team was on its way to the last day of training camp and they were in a raucous mood.

Only the junior high team had matches at another school, for the autumn city preliminaries. Eight schools were competing, and three would go on to represent that section of Tokyo for the city tournament. But Nihon Joshi had not lost a single match so far, and with only one match to go, its place in the city tournament was a done deal.

But the teammates weren't happy just because of their victories, or because they were confident that they'd win the final match. Coach Nakazawa had taken the train instead of riding the bus with them. With their annoying coach and the uptight high school students away, the junior high players were living it up.

Everyone had their cell phones out, even Sawada. Mayumi had made sure to glare at Sawada for her hypocrisy, but the older girl only winked at her. It turned out that everyone had been bringing their cell phones, despite the prohibition; Mayumi had only gotten in trouble because she'd been less sneaky about it than the others.

"Hey, Sayuri, check this out."

Sayuri peered at a sophomore girl's cell phone. "Wow, that's a love letter, isn't it? Are you sure it's okay for me to read it?"

"It's fine," said the sophomore. "Look who sent it! It's from Kamiyama, the singles player from Ginza Junior High!"

"What, that monkey?"

Both girls squealed in delight. Everyone on the bus seemed equally happy. Their faces glowed thanks to this brief moment of freedom.

In the midst of the happy crowd, Mayumi sat alone, furious.

Sawako still hadn't posted anything. Mayumi had pretended she had to go fetch more towels so she could get out of the gym yesterday during the matches, but nothing new had been posted; and she'd checked several times today, but the only entry was Mai's latest. Mayumi had been sure Sawako would post because both chapters demanded a response from her, but there had been none.

Sawako hadn't posted in four days.

What's wrong? Could something have happened to her?

Yukari hadn't posted either. And Yukari had been the one who'd set up the entire thing, so it seemed bizarre that she would suddenly get bored and drop out without a word.

The victim and the stalker have both vanished. Once Mayumi thought about it in those terms, she felt even more disturbed. *Maybe Tsunoda kidnapped Sawako.*

"Don't be silly," Mayumi muttered to herself, and caught a few curious glances from girls on the bus. *Tsunoda only exists in the world of* Chain Mail. *A fictional character can't kidnap Sawako!*

The real Sawako, Mayumi amended.

It was ironic, though, that Mayumi knew all these fictional characters better than the girls who had created them. Except for Yukari's introductory message, Mayumi's only interaction with any of them had been through the characters they'd created. Mayumi was only taking their word for it that the girls were who they said they were, or that they even existed at all.

Anyone could type the name "Mai" or "Sawako" into a blank space beside *Chain Mail's* characters. Anyone could write, "I'm a junior high freshman girl."

What if "Yukari" is a man?

Her writing style was so creepy. Would a girl really think of the sort of things she wrote? Mayumi thought back on what Yukari wrote . . .

```
Sawako just doesn't understand. I have to educate her.
It's a man's job to explain the ways of the world to
the woman he loves. Sawako might not enjoy it, but it's
something she needs.
```

```
I will achieve my goal. I will make Sawako my wife.
     I will also show that bitch detective and wimpy boyfriend
what an amazing person I am.
     To do all that, I have to watch Sawako. I can't stop
watching her, not even for a minute.
     Just as God is watching over me. God wants good people
to do good things.
     So I'll just keep watching over her. My chance to steal
her away will come.
```

Someone who read avidly and had talent could write stories entirely outside of their own experiences. By reading a lot of detective novels, doing a little online research, and using her imagination, Mayumi had been able to write as Detective Murata, even though her only real contact with the police had been asking directions when she got lost. But Murata was female, strong-willed, and absorbed by her tough job, and so Mayumi had used those points of similarity as a starting place from which to create other details.

But Yukari's stalker was male, older, insane, and dangerous. Yukari wasn't a professional writer, so how could she write so convincingly from the point of view of a character with whom she had nothing whatsoever in common?

What if "Yukari" actually is a stalker?

Mayumi had heard about men posing as boys in chat rooms to lure girls into what they assumed was an innocent teenage romance. Sometimes they posed as girls to lure other girls into what they thought were simple friendships. Porn sites catered to men with schoolgirl fetishes, and online dating sites were full of men searching for barely-legal teenagers. Mayumi had always assumed she was much too street-smart to be taken in by online strangers, but the truth was that she knew nothing about Yukari. It was quite possible that some pervert using the name Yukari had created *Chain Mail* to find schoolgirls, use it to establish a rapport with them, and then act out the events on the site.

```
Now, bride of the blood, it is your turn to prove
yourself.
    You will go on a trip with me. We will go to the promised
land together.
    I don't need to tell you what will happen if you reject
me.
```

Mayumi shivered. *Maybe I should e-mail Sawako.* She had never deleted the first e-mail she'd gotten, and that one had come directly from Sawako. If she hit "reply" to it, Sawako should get the message.

She didn't have to write a long e-mail. She could write nothing more than, "How are you doing? What's been up with you lately?"

What she wrote didn't matter. She just wanted to get a reply, so she'd know Sawako was all right. Once she got a response, even if was just "I'm fine, please don't nag me," then Mayumi could relax.

I should have e-mailed her earlier, instead of yelling at her through Detective Murata. I wonder why I never thought of that before. I guess Sawako Shinoda seems more real to me than the actual Sawako does.

Mayumi left *Chain Mail* and opened her e-mail box. She began paging down to find the message Sawako had sent her. It seemed like that had happened such a long time ago.

"Hey, Mayumi, don't you think so, too?"

"Huh? What?"

Sayuri nudged her. "What's the matter, Mayumi? You look weird. Are you bus-sick?"

"Oh, no, nothing like that." Mayumi quickly tried to mold her face into a more cheerful expression, but Sayuri was already on to her.

"I think you're working too hard," suggested Sayuri. "You don't have to do all the manager's work all by yourself. You should ask some of the seniors to help out too."

Some of the sophomore and junior girls nodded.

"Put Nagano to work. She's always cracking the whip on us, but she doesn't do anything herself."

"You should call in sick . . . For a week!"

Mayumi pretended to laugh, but she was annoyed at the triviality of the situation. These girls had it easy. All they had to worry about was winning matches and trying to get boyfriends. Meanwhile, Mayumi was busy creating one-fourth of a whole new world, and now she had to worry that a friend might be in serious trouble.

But before she could e-mail Sawako, the bus pulled up at the gym and everyone piled out. Coach Nakazawa was waiting for them inside, and he began bellowing before they even cleared the door. "Regular players, get changed and get on the courts! Freshmen, do ten laps around the field! Then get to the weight room and start working out! Go! Go! Go!"

The junior high girls, who were still tired from playing that morning, hoisted their bags and racket cases with groans. But before they could take a single step, Coach Nakazawa started yelling again. "You lazy slugs! You spent the morning goofing off, didn't you?! Well, I'm going to make you work now!" The temperature of the gym seemed to drop a degree with each word that escaped from his mouth. The girls had spent the morning playing—and winning—matches. Even though the competition hadn't been hard, it was unfair for Coach Nakazawa to accuse them of slacking off.

"Don't just stand there! Go get dressed!"

The players stomped off in chilly silence. Mayumi kept busy by disposing of used shuttlecocks, filling bottles with Pocari Sweat and passing them to the players, and running back and forth between the gym and the faucets outside to wet the washcloths that the players used to keep their hands from getting slippery with sweat.

She ran her errands without paying much attention to them, because her mind was on *Chain Mail*, Sawako, and Yukari. But she had no time to do anything about it. So she ran back and forth, getting more and more upset and frustrated with each new request made of her.

About half an hour after practice began, Coach Nakazawa called out for Mayumi. "Mayumi Hattori, get over here!"

She sprinted over to the coach.

"You're too slow!" His dark-tanned face was so close to hers that his breath blew her bangs back.

"I'm sorry!" Mayumi backed up a step.

"You don't play! You don't practice! All you do is run errands! So when I call for you, I want you to run as fast as you can! Because you have nothing else to do!"

"Yes, sir!" Mayumi stood at attention. Previous run-ins with Coach Nakazawa had taught her to stand still and erect during sessions like this. Her arms hung straight at her sides, with her middle fingers lined up exactly along the seams of her gym shorts.

"I've got an errand for you!"

"Yes, sir!"

He pulled out a folded note and waved it before her eyes. "You know where Rocket Shop Smash is? I want you to go there and order our new uniforms, twelve rolls of hand tape, and ten seven-yard rolls of racket gut string. Got it?!"

"Yes, sir!"

All right! she thought.

Rocket Shop Smash was in Shinjuku, one of Tokyo's most happening spots for teenagers and young adults. Mayumi had been sent there several times before. She was in the habit of rushing through her errands, then using the time she had left to duck into an Internet café. It charged five hundred yen per hour for unlimited use of the Internet, access to its extensive manga library, and as many cups of juice, soda, coffee, or tea as you could drink.

Mayumi had spent a number of happy hours reading her way through its collection of detective manga. Her favorite was *Case Closed,* about a brilliant detective who'd been transformed into a kid and had to keep solving mysteries. She had also recently gotten into *Master Keaton*, an action series about a single father and former SAS agent who was sent on insurance investigating adventures by Lloyd's of London.

She wouldn't be able to stay too long, but if she said that Rocket Shop Smash had been crowded, that would let her off the hook if she was an hour or so late. Then she could e-mail Sawako at her leisure, just to reassure herself that everything was all right, and also write another entry in *Chain Mail*.

"Don't lose the receipt!"

"Yes, sir!"

Mayumi unfolded the note he'd given her. It was a design for a new club uniform. The shorts and blouse were white, but tiny pink and blue roses were scattered about the shoulders and chest. "Nihon Joshi" was embroidered across the back in elegant cursive. Below that, "Tokyo" was written in a bolder hand. It was the uniform for the national tournament.

Coach Nakazawa looked at the design. For once, he didn't shout. "It's a good design, don't you think? We're using the same one for both the junior and senior high school teams."

It was so cute that Mayumi couldn't respond for a moment. "It's, um, really . . . fabulous."

The warm-up suit she was wearing had been one of last year's birthday presents from her parents. She liked its cut and color, but it was getting a little small on her, so the new uniform's arrival was perfect timing.

Despite her recent run-ins with the badminton team's authorities, Mayumi felt a surge of pride. It was good to belong to such a great team, even as the lowliest member. She grinned at the thought of wearing that snazzy uniform, and being a part of the nationally-famous Nihon Joshi Badminton Team.

As Coach Nakazawa started to walk back to the courts, Mayumi double-checked the order that had been written out below the design. Then she called out after the coach. "This order's wrong, sir! There's eight junior high freshmen, not seven."

Coach Nakazawa returned and glanced at the note. He hesitated for a moment, then said, "You're not included."

Mayumi felt a pain deep in her chest as if she had been pricked with a needle. She blinked hard.

"I mean, you don't need a uniform, right?" Coach Nakazawa seemed to be attempting a kind tone, but it sounded rusty due to lack of use. "It isn't like you'd even be on the bench at the tournaments. The other managers play too, but you don't."

"Yes, sir."

"It would be a waste to buy a uniform for you to wear when you cheer from the stands."

"Yes, sir."

"Your own gym clothes are fine."

"Yes, sir."

"You remember the conditions you accepted when you joined Nihon Joshi, right?"

"Yes, sir."

"It's not like you got in on your own merits."

"Yes, sir."

"The rest of the managers here are good enough to be star players at other schools. If they weren't, they wouldn't be able to understand what the players are going through. That's why I was against making you a manager in the first place."

"Yes, sir."

"There's no place for you on center stage here. You're not a star, and you're not going to get very far on the support staff either. You may think I'm harsh, but this is a competitor's world. People who can't handle the competition shouldn't try to push themselves onto the court."

"Yes, sir."

"So that's why you don't get a uniform. Got it?"

"Yes, sir."

"Then go!"

Mayumi was already turning away. She fled toward the exit. She thought she heard Sayuri call out from the court, but she didn't stop.

She knew that everything Coach Nakazawa had said was true. All those "yes, sirs" hadn't been sarcastic or used as the only response he'd accept. She'd known when she started that she wasn't a player and didn't belong on the team, and he'd said as much the first day he met her. She couldn't be angry at him for reminding her of the truth. But with every honest "yes, sir," the crack in her heart had grown deeper.

Mayumi realized that she was standing in front of the Kayabacho subway station. She had walked for ten minutes to get there, but she remembered nothing of her journey.

She reached into her jersey pocket to get her commuter pass and her fingers brushed against her phone.

Sawako!

Coach Nakazawa's tirade had upset her so much that she'd completely forgotten to e-mail Sawako. Mayumi logged onto the *Chain Mail* site, just in case Sawako had posted anything. But there were no new entries from her and nothing from Yukari, either.

Mayumi closed the phone with a sigh. *What in the world has happened to those two?* A story about a stalker and a girl he was stalking couldn't continue without them.

At this rate, it'll never be finished. The thought depressed her. *Chain Mail* had become her best consolation for the days of monotonous classes and nights of hard work at a sport in which she'd never excel. But it was more than a pleasant diversion, like reading a good mystery manga or treating herself to a bowl of barbecued eel over rice. For Mayumi, *Chain Mail* was . . .

What is it to me?

Her memory of Coach Nakazawa supplied the answer. "There's no place for you on center stage here."

That's it, thought Mayumi. *This story is my stage.*

She put in her commuter pass and walked through the automatic ticket gate, but she was so excited at the thought that she could barely feel the ground under her feet. She had found a place for herself. It was small and secret, but her own. *In* Chain Mail, *I can be the star. I can be as talented and valued there as Sayuri is on the court.*

"Is that thing still going on with the junior high girl?" asked a husky voice.

An old man stood in front of a newspaper kiosk. He brandished a yellowed newspaper and spoke to no one in particular. Mayumi glanced at the headline that had provoked his comment.

Junior High Freshman Girl Is Still Missing.

Mayumi stepped up to the kiosk. She had a terrible feeling of apprehension, but she could no more pass by than a nail could refuse to be drawn to a magnet. The newspapers were arranged in a tall spiraling tower, and every one of them told the same story.

A junior high freshman girl from Tokyo has been missing for four days. There has been no ransom demand.

Sawako's last entry had been four days ago.

Someone's following me.

It's a man. I don't know who he is.

I was really scared. I didn't know what to do. So I kept walking.

Mayumi remembered Yukari's earlier entry, from Tsunoda's point of view . . .

```
I will achieve my goal. I will make Sawako my wife.
My chance to steal her away will come.
```

Something large and fleshy smacked into Mayumi. She stumbled forward and lurched into the edge of the kiosk, making the newspaper tower wobble. The businessman who had run into her continued dashing for the subway without a word of apology, and the old woman running the kiosk glared at Mayumi as if it was all her fault.

"Sorry," said Mayumi. She wondered if she should buy a newspaper.

The old man pointed at the headline with a gnarled finger. "Which school is she from?"

The woman glanced at the article. "It doesn't say. They never print the details if a minor's involved."

"She must be a runaway. These evening papers blow everything out of proportion."

The woman shrugged. "I hope so. But she didn't leave a note."

Mayumi stood there indecisively, while the man and woman continued chatting. She finally decided not to buy a paper. If the article hadn't included the girl's name or any other identifying details in order to protect her privacy, there would be no way to tell if it was about Sawako.

But not knowing who it was made Mayumi even more worried.

She slowly walked away from the kiosk. Her legs traced the familiar path toward the platform for the train bound for Takadanobaba, but her mind was filled with dark thoughts.

I have to e-mail Sawako.

Mayumi sat down on a bench at the platform. She opened her e-mail folder, found the one from Sawako, and hit "reply." The text entry screen appeared.

Sawako, this is Mayumi Hattori. I play Detective Murata. Nice to meet you. Are you all right?

Mayumi paused. She was assailed by mixed feelings.

If Sawako wasn't the missing girl, but was only sick or out of town or taking a break from writing, and she got a panicky e-mail asking if she'd been kidnapped, Sawako would think Mayumi was an idiot.

And even if Mayumi hid her real concerns and just said that she had wondered why Sawako hadn't written recently and if she was okay, it wasn't clear whether e-mailing another *Chain Mail* girl was a good idea. The whole point of *Chain Mail* was that it was a break from reality. Yukari had said so explicitly in her first message, when she asked that anyone who received it should only forward it to people who were sick of the real world and wanted to escape into a fictional landscape.

So if Mayumi e-mailed Sawako for any reason, it would be an unwelcome reminder that there was no Detective Murata or Sawako Shinoda or life-and-death stakes, but rather it would point out that they were four teenage girls trying to forget their boring lives. Mayumi might not get a reply other than an e-mail from Yukari, as the site's founder and operator, scolding her for breaking the rules.

On the other hand, Mayumi couldn't stand around and do nothing.

Maybe I should ask someone else for help.

But she'd have to figure out how to do that without dragging unwelcome reality into their fragile fictional world.

Who could I ask? And how?

The train pulled up, and Mayumi automatically got on, still fiercely deep in thought. She coached herself: *You have to think of something! You have to take action!*

Then she heard a voice in her mind, one that seemed to belong to an older, more confident Mayumi (perhaps the woman she might become one day): *There's no one who can do this but you, so you'd better pull yourself together. You can do it. You're the star.*

Smiling to herself, Mayumi began to type.

MAI
MONDAY, OCTOBER 13, 4:03 PM.
YOTSUYA TRAIN STATION.

Mai walked past the Yotsuya subway station, and headed for the train station instead. She was on her way to a Black Thunder concert at a club in Meguro, which was only one stop away on the subway line. If she used the train, the trip would be much longer and more indirect. But she had a student commuter card, so she could ride the train for free. She was still trying not to spend her parents' money, and was willing to go out of her way to do so.

The train arrived just as Mai stepped onto the platform. It was a holiday evening, and not many people were headed to Meguro. There weren't any seats open, but there weren't many people standing either.

They all glanced at her as she boarded the train. Mai was dressed entirely in black: tank top, fake fur jacket, leather shorts, knee-high socks, and platform shoes. Her eyelids were smudged with black eye shadow, and when she stared back at the passengers through her mascara-laden lashes, they all hastily looked away.

But Mai hadn't dressed like that to look tough. She wore black because Black Thunder wore black. Everyone had darkness hidden deep in their souls, but most people pretended it wasn't there. Black Thunder laid it out honestly for all to see. Their lyrics spoke of witches, black magic, and monsters, and celebrated beauty and terror. They dressed to match their themes, and Mai dressed to match them.

She recalled with annoyance how some girls claimed that Black Thunder's brilliant lead singer, Maya, was only copying the androgynous singer Gackt from his Goth phase, when he'd been with Malice Mizer. Other girls, who were fans of boring bands that wore street clothes and sang clichéd love songs, turned up their noses at the genius that was Black Thunder and said things like, "Who cares about J-rock any more? Those idol singers on TV are so much cuter."

But Mai wasn't swayed by peer pressure. Those teen idols were like cheap candy that you throw to kids. They made money for the adults who created them to match some current trend, but they melted away with the passage of time.

Black Thunder would never fade. The musicians didn't concern themselves with what sort of music was popular, but only with what was deep and true. Black Thunder was timeless. No—Black Thunder was beyond timeless. For two hours on stage, Black Thunder created a whole other dimension.

Black Thunder makes their own time and space. And then they surround us with it, and blot out this soiled world.

Mai suddenly felt someone watching her. She looked up. Two middle-aged men in a corner of the compartment were leering at her.

Old perverts! she thought angrily. That sort of thing was exactly what made the world a nasty, depressing place.

She glared at them until they lowered their eyes. Then, holding onto the handrail, she pulled her cell phone out of her black leather purse. *Chain Mail* was a perfect escape for times like these. She would enjoy having Kouhei confront Tsunoda.

Mai hoped that Sawako had posted since the last time she'd checked the site. Mayumi, the girl playing the detective, had seemed quite worried about her.

But there was no new entry from Sawako. Only Mayumi had posted. It had been four days since anyone but Mayumi or Mai had written anything. Mai began to read, but a sense of foreboding replaced her usual thrill of anticipation.

DATE AND TIME: OCTOBER 13, 3:41 PM
AUTHOR: MAYUMI
CHARACTER: DETECTIVE MURATA

Detective Murata got into her car. She had finished gathering information on a purse-snatching case, and she was looking forward to a bento box for dinner and a long hot bath. But before she started the engine, she opened her cell phone.

She had three new e-mails. All of them were from other detectives—two communiqués summarizing their progress on other cases, and one reporting that the vending machine inside the office still refused to dispense hot coffee. There was no word from Sawako.

It had been four days since Murata had been able to get in touch with Sawako. There hadn't been any phone calls from Kouhei, either.

"What's going on?" exclaimed Murata. "Why won't they respond?" She punched the steering wheel as if she could beat an answer out of it.

She had swung by Tsunoda's apartment earlier that day, but he wasn't there. The stalker had an uncanny ability to guess when Murata might show up—even when she tried showing up past midnight, he wasn't in. His apartment manager claimed that he hadn't moved out . . . but for all intents and purposes, he'd vanished.

There had been no contact with Sawako and no sign of Tsunoda, either. Murata wasn't sure what to do.

Sawako's disappearing act didn't necessarily mean that Tsunoda had gotten her. She'd been trying to keep the situation a secret from her social-climbing parents, but no matter how uptight they were about preserving the façade that they were respectable people who would never need to call the police, if their teenage daughter hadn't come home in four days, they'd have been all over the police station like white on rice. Since she hadn't been reported missing, Murata figured her parents must know where she was.

But something wasn't right.

Murata had no proof that anything had gone wrong in the last four days, but her intuition was screaming louder than the siren on her car. And that same intuition had cracked many a tough case. Murata had absolute confidence in her instincts. If she felt like something was wrong, then something was wrong.

She had to take action.

Kouhei! Murata thought. *If I can meet up with Kouhei, the two of us should be able to figure out a plan of attack.*

They could pool their knowledge of Sawako, and use it to find her and figure out why she'd dropped out of contact. And then they could continue helping her to evade and, eventually, capture her stalker.

But they'd have to be cautious. Tsunoda had proved that he could spy on Sawako's activities and whereabouts.

Murata and Kouhei had to assume that he was equally capable of keeping tabs on them. If they did anything to attract Tsunoda's attention or incite him in any way, there was no telling what he might do.

Murata was a police officer and she'd accepted the risks that came with her profession from the moment she first pinned on her badge.

But Sawako and Kouhei were civilians. If anything happened to them because Murata made an error of judgment, she would never forgive herself.

She needed to meet up with Kouhei somewhere safe from Tsunoda and his binoculars.

A movie theatre? she wondered. *No, then we wouldn't be able to talk. Kouhei's house?*

That was no good either. Tsunoda undoubtedly hated Kouhei as a possible rival for Sawako's affections.

He probably knew where Kouhei lived, and might even have staked it out, waiting for Kouhei to come home so he could attack him.

Murata smacked her fist against the steering wheel again. "Got it!" she exclaimed.

They could go to an Internet café. A number of them had recently installed double seats and lowered the lights to attract courting couples.

Even if Tsunoda followed Kouhei there, once Kouhei sat down and pulled the curtain across the door of the booth, Tsunoda would have to go away or else attract suspicion.

Mai looked up from the phone and tilted her head to the side as she thought about the post she read.

It almost seemed as if someone else had written it under Mayumi's name. It was in Mayumi's typical hard-boiled style, but the point of view was different. Normally she wrote from Detective Murata's point of view in first person, but this entry was in third person.

The plot was strange too. Mayumi's posts were normally ultra-realistic. Her detective acted like a real police officer: direct, logical, and to the point. Detective Murata's actions never failed to make sense. So why in the world would she decide that seeing Kouhei in person was so important that she had to set up an elaborate meeting in an Internet café, when it would be so much easier to telephone him? Also, in Mai's last entry, she had sent Kouhei to Sawako's house. So if Murata was so worried about Sawako, why wouldn't she call Kouhei immediately and ask him if Sawako had been home?

Mai went back the entry, but the next plot twist was even more bizarre. As Mai read on, she could feel her eyebrows arching in disbelief. Mayumi had Detective Murata drive out to Kouhei's university and leave a note for him in his shoe.

They don't even have shoe lockers in college.

University students, unlike junior and senior high schoolers, wore their shoes to class. Mai knew that because her school, Shirogane Preparatory, was next to Shirogane University. But even if Mayumi had never been inside a college, her entries were always carefully researched. She normally wouldn't describe anything in real life that she hadn't checked for accuracy.

And come on . . . a note in a shoe?!

The whole scene read as if it had been lifted out of some kids' adventure story. Mai couldn't believe Mayumi would write anything that silly. *Could she have a little brother who had logged on to her account and written an entry for her?*

Mai continued reading, alert for further inconsistencies. The next part was just the text of the note that Murata left inside Kouhei's left sneaker.

Take the southeast exit out of the Shinjuku train station. There's a GAP store to your left. A video arcade is across the street from the GAP. An Internet café called Access is on the fourth floor of the building with the video arcade. You can take the elevator from the entrance next to the arcade. Wait for me in booth D-12.

That was the end of the post. Mai looked up with a sigh.

That's an awfully detailed set of directions.

Mayumi was good at using precise details to make her entries sound real. Her metaphors were vivid, too. Mai thought that Mayumi was probably used to writing, and definitely read more books than Mai did. But the level of detail in the note to Kouhei seemed excessive and inappropriate for fiction. Mayumi's posts usually got right to the point, rather than going on and on about elevators and booth numbers.

Even apart from the weird note, nothing in this entry felt right. Murata's sense of being backed into a corner came through loud and clear, but other than that, it didn't read like a story.

It read like a message. *A message in code.*

Mai scrolled up the page and started reading the post from the beginning.

It seemed as if Mayumi was doing the talking, not Murata. Mai tried reading it again with Mayumi's name in place of Murata's. That made a lot more sense. And then, if she replaced all the characters' names with their authors' names . . . Then Mayumi clearly wanted to meet up with Mai to pool their knowledge of Sawako and figure out why she'd dropped out of contact.

Mai blinked at the screen. It was hard to believe at first, but when she reread the post once more, she became convinced of it.

That would explain the hyper-detailed directions to the Internet café. Tokyo was a big and confusing city. It wasn't laid out on a grid like New York—it was full of dead-ends, winding roads, and narrow alleys. Most of its streets had neither names nor numbers, and the buildings were numbered in order of which had been built first, rather than which was the first on the block. The officers who manned the police boxes that were stationed every couple of blocks spent most of their time giving out directions to lost tourists and locals alike—and directions to anything other than a major landmark had to be given in precise detail. If Mayumi really wanted to meet Mai, the careful notes about the elevator and the southeast exit made perfect sense.

And if Mayumi had gone to that much trouble, it seemed a shame to let her down.

The train pulled into Shinjuku station. Mai exited and stepped out of the way of the surging crowds. She was tempted by the stairway that led down to the platform where she could catch the Meguro train to the club where her beloved Black Thunder would play. But, allowing herself just one regretful glance, she turned her back on that and walked along the platform toward the southeast exit.

In her mind, another Mai began talking. *That* Mai was also dressed in black, but her leather was real and her makeup wasn't smudged and she wore expensive contact lenses that gave her bright green eyes with slit pupils like a cat's. That Mai would have been the coolest person at any Black Thunder concert.

Her voice was low and sexy.

You haven't forgotten that you're saving your money, have you? purred the cooler version of Mai. *If you spend your money at the net café, you won't be able to afford the cover charge at the club. Do you really want to miss Black Thunder just to sit in a net café like a geek, looking for a message that probably won't even be there, from some Internet pal who might not even be who she says she is?*

Mai hated the thought of missing Black Thunder at all, and it would be even worse to miss them because she'd misinterpreted the post. For all she knew, Mayumi hadn't intended to send her a coded message at all, and this was just a wild goose chase.

I've never met Sawako or Yukari, let alone Mayumi. How can I trust what they write?

Even if Mayumi and Mai did meet and they did decide that Sawako was in trouble, what could two junior high girls possibly do to help another junior high girl when they didn't even know her full name?

Here in overcrowded, trendy Shinjuku, crimes were committed every minute. Pickpockets preyed on tourists, drunken businessmen and angry teenagers got into fights, and gangs shook down small businesses for protection money. The police were busy with real complaints about real crimes. Mai imagined talking to a cop, saying something like, "I've never met this girl, but she's stopped e-mailing me, so I think she might have been kidnapped by a stalker. I think her first name is Sawako, but that could be a pen name." There was no way the police would take her seriously.

Go to the club! urged the cooler Mai.

But . . . thought Mai. *That last entry . . .*

In Mai's mind, every line where Mayumi had written "Kouhei" had been replaced with a line reading "Mai." The post had transformed itself into an urgent letter from an old friend.

Mayumi told me that she wants to meet me, replied Mai to the cooler Mai in her head. *I can't just ignore her.*

If they couldn't go to the police, they'd work together to protect Sawako from the stalker. Between the two of them, they could accomplish anything—as long as Mai held up her end.

It was the first time Mai had ever felt that way about a friend.

Friend? Cool Mai exclaimed tauntingly. *How can you call her a friend? You've never even met her.*

Shut up! Mai snapped. She put her commuter pass through the automatic ticket gate and went outside. The crowded sidewalks and ad-plastered buildings of Shinjuku spread out before her.

The stairwell she ascended was covered in posters and leaflets. A homeless man clutching a brown paper bag staggered by and almost collided with her. A high school girl in a sailor uniform leaned against the wall, snuggling up to a guy in dreadlocks, and a girl in a plain blue school jersey hurried past them. A taxi pushed its way through the wave of people who had overflowed on to the street.

The GAP store was exactly where Mayumi had said it would be. And across the street was the video arcade.

"There it is!" yelped Mai.

A man in a black silk shirt and a heavy gold chain turned and gave her a lecherous glance from overtop his sunglasses. But Mai was so excited that the arcade really existed that she didn't even bother to glare at him.

Photo booths and UFO catchers, as well as video games, were visible through the glass walls of the arcade. A residential building was next door to it, and an elevator nestled between them. A sign near the elevator read, *"Access Internet Café: 4th Floor."*

Mai was definitely in the right place.

She slowly walked across the street. As she got closer, she was barraged by the beeps, gunshots, screams, explosions, screeching tires, and theme songs of the video games. But the pounding of her heart drowned out most of the noise.

As if in a dream, she got into the elevator and rode it to the fourth floor. When she stepped out, she was inside Access.

The woman at the front desk wore a white blouse and gray vest. "Welcome! Would you like a smoking or non-smoking seat?"

How could anyone think Mai was old enough to smoke? "Non—" she began, then remembered that Mayumi had written that a seat would be reserved. "Um, is D-12 available?"

The woman eyed Mai from beneath her bangs for a moment. Just as Mai wondered if the woman had completely spaced out, she spoke. "D-12 is a double seat. Where's your companion?"

Mai was thrown for a moment, then remembered that Detective Murata had planned to share a double seat with Kouhei.

"He—she—they'll be arriving after me, I think," Mai stammered. The woman's eyes were blue. *Color contacts,* she guessed. They gave her eyes an intimidating, icy gloss. It unnerved Mai.

"Coffee and tea is available at the drink bar," the blue-eyed clerk said abruptly. "Take whatever you like. If you want any DVDs or games, ask for them here at the front desk. The bill will be—oh, here, just take it." She thrust a clipboard into Mai's hands, then vanished into a back room.

Mai was left alone. Her receipt was clipped to the top of the clipboard.

What was with that weird clerk? Can't anything be normal today?

She helped herself to a green tea latte and carried it with her as she ventured farther into the café. Bookshelves packed with magazines and manga loomed as high and close together as a bamboo forest. The computer stations were behind the bookcases. Booths were partitioned off like the study room in a library. But some of the computers had black loveseats instead of regular chairs, and the lights were very dim. It was probably supposed to be romantic, but in Mai's current state of mind it seemed eerie instead.

Most of the booths had the curtains drawn back, unoccupied. She glanced at her watch. It was almost 5:40 PM; too early for people who'd come after work, and probably too late for the ones who's skipped work or school that day.

D-12 was the farthest booth in. D-11 through D-16 were all doubles with tiny loveseats that were only a little wider than the regular chairs. All of them were empty.

She sat down in booth D-12. "Now, then . . ." she murmured to herself, then trailed off into silence.

The reading lamp in the booth only illuminated the top half of her body, which made the room seem creepy. Mai twitched nervously, and her hand reflexively landed on top of the computer mouse. The mouse shifted, and the dark monitor lit up and displayed instructions for using the computer.

Her agitation was soothed by the familiar white light of the computer screen. She wondered if Mayumi was going to show up. Everything had been exactly as the note had said, but that didn't mean that it had actually been a message directed at *her*. Mayumi could have simply been describing a place she knew well.

Told you so, said Cool Mai. *That was fiction, you idiot. It wasn't real. Remember that first e-mail? "Would you like to create a fictional world?" Now you've missed the chance to see Black Thunder. Moron.*

Mai didn't have a good response to that. Her motives in coming here were sketchy. Had she wanted to see Mayumi for the thrill of meeting the person who had created Detective Murata, or in the hope of making a new friend? Or had she only wanted to learn the truth about Sawako's disappearance?

Well, if Mayumi doesn't show up, then that means that she wasn't really worried about Sawako, and that means probably nothing happened to Sawako and I imagined the whole thing. So if Mayumi doesn't come, that's actually a good thing.

But Mai had been so excited at the thought of meeting Mayumi. When she'd found Access, it was as if she was in her own adventure. Even seeing Black Thunder live felt dull in comparison.

But Mayumi wasn't here. Mai's disappointment mingled with anger—at Mayumi for not showing up and at herself for having been stupid enough to expect anything. Part of her wanted to stomp out, and part of her was afraid that if she left, Mayumi would come running into the café just as Mai got on the train to come back home.

Mai's hand slipped on the mouse. She was so tense that her palms were sweating.

"Maybe I'll read some manga," she said aloud. She'd already paid, so she might as well finish her latte, read a little, and give Mayumi a chance to arrive.

Just as she decided to catch up on *Death Note*, she felt a tingle along her spine. Someone was standing behind her.

"Want to play?"

Mai twisted around. A young man in a suit was leaning against the back of her sofa. His hair was stiffened into a pompadour, and the light of the reading lamp bounced off his glasses, making them opaque. The glowing circles of his glasses and his angular face reminded Mai of a praying mantis. "What?"

The mantis-dude smirked at her. "I know you're sending men e-mail for some online dating scheme. Why don't you play with me instead?" As he leaned in closer, the sickly scent of the cologne he was drenched in wafted over her.

"That's not what I'm doing!" yelled Mai, jumping to her feet. Then she remembered that she was dressed for a Black Thunder concert. No wonder the woman at the front desk had been so hostile. She probably thought Mai had come in alone and asked for a double seat so she could send out lures for men at dating sites, then meet her sugar daddies here.

A wave of blood rushed to her face, making her cheeks feel hot and swollen. How dare they all judge her based on the way she looked?! They didn't know anything about her.

"Why don't you go play with yourself, you loser?!" shouted Mai. She was amazed at the power and volume of her own voice. Everyone in the café had to be watching her though she couldn't see them in the dim light. "Go on! Go feel up your keyboard, because that's the only thing that'll ever let you touch it!"

The mantis-dude slunk away.

Mai grabbed her bag and receipt, and shoved back the sofa. It was heavier than she had expected and her knee smacked against the computer table. The keyboard fell off, but its cable stopped it from hitting the floor. It hung in midair, slowly revolving.

Mai picked it up. It had a yellow strip stuck to its underside—a long, thin post-it note. It was covered in tiny letters that looked like black sesame seeds.

To Mai,
Please e-mail me. I would like to talk about Sawako.
Mayumi

Mai clutched the post-it in both hands, reading it over and over. The thrill was back.

MAYUMI

MONDAY, OCTOBER 13, 6:15 PM.

NIHON JOSHI ACADEMY GYMNASIUM.

"Where the hell have you been?!" shouted Coach Nakazawa.

When the echoes of his voice died down, the squeaks of shoes on polished wood, the thwacks of shuttlecocks being hit, and the shouts of players encouraging each other all fell silent. An eerie quiet descended upon the gym.

The coach spun around. "Why are you stopping? This has nothing to do with you! Play on!"

"Sorry!" yelled the girls, and the normal gym soundtrack resumed.

Coach Nakazawa turned back to loom over Mayumi. "You left at two. It takes half an hour maximum to get to Shinjuku. Even if you spent an hour at the racket shop, you still should have been back by four."

Mayumi stared at the floor while the coach ranted at her. She had polished that floor almost every day for the last six months, but it was still covered in scratches and streaks of black rubber.

"So what time is it now?" Coach Nakazawa bellowed. "It's six! Six o'clock! There's only fifteen minutes of training to go! And you know what that means, don't you?"

This wasn't going at all the way Mayumi had planned. She'd known Coach Nakazawa would be angry with her for being late, but she'd had no idea he'd be this scary. She was so intimidated.

"You don't, huh?" Coach Nakazawa thrust a meaty finger in her face. "Well, I know. It means that while your classmates and seniors were training hard, you were slacking off in Shinjuku!"

Coach Asano, the slender woman who led the high school team, stepped in. She took Mayumi gently by the shoulders. "So, you're finally back. What happened? We were worried about you."

The knots of tension in Mayumi's back began to relax, but Coach Nakazawa was still standing right in front of her—red faced and eyes bulging. Mayumi swallowed.

"Please tell us the truth," said Coach Asano. "If you answer us honestly, we won't yell at you. Promise."

Mayumi would have liked to confide in Coach Asano. But she wasn't about to explain that she'd gone to an Internet café because she was worried about an e-mail pen-pal, which had accounted for half an hour, or that deciding how to leave a secret message for another e-mail pen-pal had taken another half-hour, or that the final hour of lateness had been caused by the presence of the latest volume of *Kindaichi Case Files.*

"Um, Miss Jinnai . . ." Though her voice came out in a nervous squeak, Mayumi was relieved that she was able to speak at all.

" 'Miss Jinai'?" echoed Coach Asano.

"Kimiko Jinnai," said Mayumi in more assured tones. "She was in Racket Shop Smash doing an interview with a talk show . . ."

This happened to be true. Kimiko Jinnai (a former Olympic badminton player turned sportscaster), had indeed been in Rocket Shop Smash, thereby relieving Mayumi of the need to make up a cover story. Mayumi had been excited by the glimpse she caught of a celebrity she'd only ever seen on TV and in magazines before, but rather than taking a place among the swarming fans who were watching the interview, she made her purchases, placed her orders, and continued on to Access.

"I see. And you were so excited to see her that you just couldn't tear yourself away, right?" Coach Asano smiled conspiratorially, as if she too would have dawdled to stay in the presence of a star.

But the mention of the badminton star only made Coach Nakazawa angrier. "You got caught up watching Kimiko Jinnai?

What do you care about her? You don't *play* badminton!" Now that he'd gotten warmed up, his voice was loud enough to make the windows rattle. "I'd have liked to have heard an interview with a great player like Kimiko Jinnai! I'd have liked to have everyone hear it—I mean, everyone but *you!* It would have been inspiring for them! But no amount of inspiration will ever make you a good player! That interview was *wasted* on you!"

"Coach Nakazawa!" Coach Asano, who had been trying to get a word in earlier, finally managed to break in. "That's enough."

"Please keep out of this, Coach Asano," said Coach Nakazawa, glaring. "Mayumi, you don't need to stand around getting tips from Olympic athletes, because you're not an athlete. If you've got time on your hands, come here and help pick up shuttlecocks, wash the players' uniforms, and fix them boxed lunches. That's the kind of work you're suited for."

Cooking, laundry, and fetch-and-carry, thought Mayumi miserably. *It's true that I can do all that, and I can't play badminton.*

Coach Nakazawa went on, "That's why you came to this school. We only let you in because you said you'd help the team behind the scenes."

But that's not why I came here, she thought. *I came to be with Sayuri, not to be the all-purpose slave of the junior high badminton team.*

"If you can't make yourself useful, then quit. Quit the team and quit the school."

Coach Asano said, "Coach Nakazawa, you're going too far."

"No, I'm finally going far enough. A girl who skips out on training to gawk at celebrities in Shinjuku isn't a girl I want on my team. She's not a real player, and it's better for her if she stops pretending that she is."

Coach Nakazawa, whose nickname was "The Brown Bear" stood threateningly over Coach Asano. He was twice her weight, though she was tall, and he looked as if he could pick her up and break her over his knee. But luckily she was much stronger than she seemed.

"Coach Nakazawa," said Coach Asano firmly. "I will not allow anyone to say things that will hurt the children. Not even you."

Nakazawa's bloodshot eyes narrowed. "No pain, no gain. We'll never win the championship if we baby the players."

"If we have to emotionally scar the children to make them win, then winning's not worth it."

"Why don't you drop that stale 'good cop' routine? The players are here because they want to win. What'll really scar them is losing."

Mayumi buried her head in her hands. She hated being between two people who were fighting, and it was worse when they were fighting over her.

I didn't come here to run errands, she thought. *I came here because I thought Sayuri needed me, and I didn't want to be separated from her. And Sayuri does need me! She said she wouldn't come here unless I did, too. But . . .*

"Mayumi!"

Mayumi dropped her arms and looked up.

Coach Asano patted her on the shoulder. "It seems that Coach Nakazawa and I don't agree about your potential. So I'm bringing you over to the high school team. That'll be a much better fit for you. Just you wait; between you and me, we'll make you the best team manager in Japan."

But that's not what I wanted . . .

Coach Nakazawa let out a disgusted grunt. "Fine with me. Sayuri Sano's on a plateau, and I think it's because she relies so much on Mayumi. I've always wanted to separate the two of them. Without that crutch, I'm sure Sayuri's game will improve."

Mayumi detested Coach Nakazawa, but she'd never thought he was stupid, especially when it came to badminton. *Could it be true that I'm holding Sayuri back? How can having a good friend at her side be bad for Sayuri?*

Coach Asano gave Coach Nakazawa an ironic smile. "How unusual. For once I completely agree. That makes it easier. Mayumi, please get your things together; we're going to the high school right now."

I don't want to go! Mayumi thought frantically. *I don't want to stay on a team where the coach hates me, but I don't want to leave Sayuri either!*

"Hurry up and get her out of here," snapped Coach Nakazawa. "I don't want anyone in this gym who doesn't belong here."

"I can't believe you feel comfortable saying that to a child."

Coach Asano's kindness was suddenly more than Mayumi could stand. She pulled away from the woman and dashed out of the gym.

"Wait!" yelled Coach Asano as loud as Coach Nakazawa but less harsh.

"Mayumi!" called a far-off voice that sounded like Sayuri's.

But Mayumi didn't stop. She skidded around the corner of the building and wound up in the strip between the gym and the apartment building. She sat down on the asphalt, trying not to cry.

Coach Nakazawa and Coach Asano words echoed in her mind . . .

She's not a real player, and it's better for her if she stops pretending that she is.

We'll make you the best team manager in Japan.

Tears ran down Mayumi's cheeks, leaving streaks of warmth in their wake. "But that's not what I want," she said softly. Then she screamed, "That's not what I want!"

Mayumi got up and ran past the gym and through the deserted schoolyard. In her left hand, she clutched her cell phone.

MAI

MONDAY, OCTOBER 13, 10:33 PM.

YOTSUYA, SUBDIVISION 3, MAI'S ROOM.

Mai clicked "refresh," for about the five hundredth time. The computer screen went to blue, then reset. No new messages.

As soon as she had returned from Access, she had reset her home computer to check for new messages every minute, and turned up the sound so a bell would signal their arrival. It was compulsive and neurotic to keep hitting refresh, but she couldn't help it.

Click.

No new messages.

"Then why did you drag me out there?" snapped Mai, as if the computer might start speaking in Mayumi's voice. "Why leave a message if you won't respond?"

Mai had e-mailed Mayumi from her cell phone as soon as she'd left Access.

MONDAY, OCTOBER 13, 4:33 PM.

This is Mai. I play "Kouhei." I got your e-mail address (obviously!) What do you think we should do? Do you think something's happened to Sawako?

Mai had written the message as she'd walked down Shinjuku's crowded streets, so absorbed that she'd walked into people a couple of times. She started paying more attention to where she was going after she collided with a *yakuza*. No one else but a gangster would wear sunglasses and a white suit. He cursed at her until her stammered apologies finally satisfied him, then he turned away with a sneer. Mai figured that since her e-mail to Mayumi led her to a literal run-in with a gangster, the least Mayumi could do was write back . . .

MONDAY, OCTOBER 13, 5:47 PM.

It's Mai again. I heard on the news that a junior high freshman girl is missing. Do you think it could be Sawako? Please contact me.

Mai had written that e-mail after she'd gotten home. She was eager to get in touch with Mayumi and it took too long to type on the tiny keys of her cell phone, so she booted up the computer to send her second message.

MONDAY, OCTOBER 13, 6:51 PM.

It's Mai again. I'm sorry to keep bothering you, but I'm really worried. Do you think we should call the police? I'm waiting for you to write back.

She had sent that e-mail from her home computer too, and when she reread it, she wondered if Mayumi would be able to sense the anger and frustration buried beneath the apology.

Mai had spent the entire evening in front of the computer. Her mother had popped in to cheerfully tell her that she was going out. "Your father and I are going to a Kabuki performance. Sorry to leave you here, but you don't like Kabuki, do you? Besides, it's a date. We've been planning it for a while . . . Actually, I didn't think you'd be home this early."

Her mother had seemed unusually cheerful as she'd bustled around the room, telling Mai she'd left a beef stroganoff dinner in the freezer and reminding her to call if there was an emergency. Mai suspected that her mother's long-awaited romantic evening was only part of the reason she seemed so pleased with the world. Her mother had started beaming the moment she'd seen Mai doing research on the Internet, instead of out clubbing. Tonight she was home by herself, and that made her mother happy.

No matter how much lip service her mother gave to the idea that teenagers needed to have their own private lives away from their parents' watchful eyes, she did care what sort of private life Mai led. She wanted Mai to act like a good little junior high school girl, the sort who studied every night and loved wearing her school uniform. Why else would she go on and on about how much she trusted and respected her daughter, and then look pleased as punch when Mai came home before sundown?

But Mai couldn't work up a good head of steam over her mother's hypocrisy tonight. Tonight, all of Mai's worries were focused on the *Chain Mail* girls.

Half of her was afraid that she was overreacting and making herself look ridiculous, and the other half was terrified that Sawako was the missing girl who'd been mentioned on TV. One moment she worried that Yukari could be a victim as well, and the next moment she worried that Yukari might really be a stalker.

"What am I doing?!" yelled Mai, hitting the keyboard with both hands. The sound of her voice echoed through the empty house. Onscreen, a line of gibberish appeared in an open e-mail box. The empty beef stroganoff container, the contents of which Mai had eaten while sitting in front of the computer, fell off the table.

And what's up with Mayumi? Why would she go to so much trouble to get me her e-mail address, then never write back?

Unless . . . I've been sitting here checking my e-mail, but I haven't checked Chain Mail *since I got on the train to Access. Maybe Mayumi hasn't e-mailed me because she decided she'd rather communicate through* Chain Mail *after all.*

Chain Mail loaded much faster on the computer than it did on her cell phone.

There was one new entry.

"I knew it!" exclaimed Mai.

Click.

DATE AND TIME: MONDAY, OCTOBER 13, 10:03 PM
AUTHOR: SAWAKO
CHARACTER: SAWAKO SHINODA

Mai gasped. Sawako had returned! Sawako, who'd been missing for four days.

That explained why Mayumi had never replied: they'd wanted to talk about Sawako, but it looked like Sawako had spoken for herself. Mai hastily scrolled down the page.

Everything was dark. It was so dark that I had to blink a few times before I could tell if my eyes were open or closed.

Where was I?

I felt so disoriented.

I tried to focus on what I knew.

It was pitch black. I thought I was sitting down, but I was so dizzy that I couldn't be sure. I don't know how I knew, but I was sure that I wasn't at home. So where was I?

What had happened?

I began to remember . . .

After school was over, I had gotten on a train with some friends. But after a few transfers, I was alone.

It had been about seven in the evening when I'd gotten off the train. I ambled along the roundabout in front of the station, bought a grilled mackerel bento at a convenience store, and then walked until I came to a wooded area.

Something hit me hard on the back of my head.

Then . . . I'm not sure what happened, but I remember a clammy hand grabbing my arm.

"I've finally got you," said a strange voice. It was high-pitched, but it didn't sound like a woman's.

It was too dark to see anything, but the voice seemed to be coming from somewhere directly in front of me. A breeze blew my bangs aside. Or maybe it was a puff of breath on my face. But it was so cold. Surely a person's breath couldn't be that cold.

"Who's th-there?" My voice got caught in my throat, and the words didn't come out clearly.

"I'm your guardian angel."

Guardian angel? Then *he* had caught me. I screamed.

"Don't bother." He laughed. "Don't cry, either. No one can hear you. The only one who can hear you now is the only one who's *worthy* of hearing your voice. That's me, your guardian angel." He started panting very heavily.

I was sure it was his breath I'd felt on my face, but it was so cold, and it smelled like damp earth.

"You don't have to be afraid. I won't hurt you. I just want you to be by my side. I'm going to keep you safe, like the precious treasure you are. Safe with me, where no one else can touch you, forever and ever and ever . . ."

I heard his high-pitched cackle, and a door slammed.

And then . . . I'm not sure what happened then. Either he drugged me or I fainted.

When I woke up, I was alone in the dark.

I could smell mildew and grass. The air felt damp and clean. I didn't think I was in a real house. It had to be some kind of shack.

And from the smell of the air, it was probably way out in the mountains somewhere.

I tried to stand, and that was when I realized that I was tied up. I was sitting in a splintered wooden chair. Both of my arms were tied behind my back, and more ropes wound around my waist. I strained against them, but they cut into my flesh. It hurt.

I started to panic.

I screamed and thrashed about like a fish on a line. The chair creaked and rocked, and almost fell over.

I stopped moving, then wriggled carefully. One of the chair's arms wobbled. If I kept struggling, the chair might come apart, and then the ropes would fall off.

I started to struggle again, but I didn't scream. I kicked with my legs, then rocked my shoulders back and forth. The ropes burned as they moved against my skin, but I clenched my teeth and kept trying.

Creak . . . If I could break the chair, I'd be free. So that chair was going to break, dammit!

Crack! The back broke away from the seat—it sounded like a bone snapping.

I collapsed to the ground. My arms were still tied, so I couldn't prevent my right hip and shoulder from slamming into the floor.

I quickly struggled out of the tethered ropes. Then I shakily stood up, though my eyes watered with pain.

Suddenly I heard footsteps.

He was on the other side of the door.

I grabbed a broken chunk of the chair and crept toward the sound of the footsteps. It was dark, but I felt for the wall, and then I pressed myself beside the door.

Creak . . .

A ray of faint gray light entered the room.

"What's the matter?" It was his voice. "If you stay with me, there's nothing to be afraid of."

I jumped into the light. My eyes hurt after so long in the dark, and I couldn't see anything clearly. But I swung my weapon as hard as I could toward that hateful voice.

There was a crunch, and then a gurgling wail of agony.

I dropped the board, slipped past the howling figure in the doorway, and dashed away from my prison.

A damp and chilly wind blew past my cheeks. It was night, but my eyes began to adjust to the starlight. I was in a grassy glen, and the shack I had escaped from was now a black silhouette behind me.

A shrill moan emanated from the shack. "My eyes! My eyes!"

When I had hit him with the board, there had been a crunch on impact, immediately followed by a feeling that the wood had sunk into something soft.

"Ugh!" I shuddered.

Then I realized that the sound I'd made might have given my position away. I ran into the forest. Leaves and twigs lashed my face, and branches raked my bare arms. But I barely felt the pain; I was so intent on my escape.

I don't know where I went, or how long I ran. I kept forcing myself to go forward, and eventually the trees were gone. The ground dropped away from beneath my feet. I tumbled down a grassy slope and collided into some sort of wall at the bottom.

I staggered to my feet and looked around. The light was much brighter here because there were streetlamps. I was standing in a small valley. There was a big road sign nearby. I had fallen against the road's guard rail.

Then I heard the sound of an engine. When I turned, I could see headlights in the distance.

The engine quickly got louder and louder—the car was coming fast. If I jumped out, it might hit me . . . but if I didn't, I'd be stranded.

I had to get help. And I'd rather die quickly than be locked up again in his cabin.

I leapt out into the middle of the road, waving my arms frantically. I could see nothing but white light; rainbows danced around the edge of my vision.

Brakes squealed, then screeched, louder and louder. The wind buffeted me, but I held my ground.

Then the night was silent. The lights turned off.

Blinking against the purple after-images, I saw that the car had stopped in front of me. Its silver bumper was an inch away from my skirt.

"Please save me!" I cried.

The driver stared at me. His mouth hung open in shock.

I could see my reflection in the windshield—a shadowy translucent figure.

My face and arms were red and black with blood and dirt, and my sailor uniform was crumpled and covered in green grass stains. My hair was wild, half-covering my face.

But I had no time to worry about that. I banged on the passenger seat window with both hands. "Please, please, if you won't let me in, at least call the police! You have to call Detective Murata!"

That was so powerful, thought Mai.

She had always thought the other three girls were good writers. They all managed to create entries that were entertaining and also carried the story forward. But this post struck Mai as something special. It amazed her that a junior high school girl could write something that scary and suspenseful.

It also amazed her that Sawako had written that *much*. None of them had written more than a few pages before, but the kidnapping entry was long enough to be a novel chapter. *She must have written it on a computer. It would have taken forever to type out all those pages on a cell phone. It's like all her writing energy was trapped for four days, and then it came out in a waterfall*, she thought.

Mai smiled. Sawako was back.

After all that worry and secret agent business with the Internet café, Sawako had returned unharmed. Well, unharmed wasn't quite the right word, since nothing had happened to her in the first place. She obviously hadn't been the missing girl or she wouldn't have just sat down and continued her story after a four-day disappearance.

It was a weird coincidence though, that when Mai had been worried about Sawako getting kidnapped, Sawako decided to have Tsunoda kidnap her character.

But it *was* a coincidence. Abduction was the next logical step in the story. It was silly of Mai to have gotten so freaked out over Sawako's absence. What were the odds of someone Mai knew getting kidnapped? It must've been one in a million.

Maybe I shouldn't feel so stupid, thought Mai. *Mayumi was worried, too. I bet she's feeling just as embarrassed as I am now.*

That explained why Mayumi had never written back. She must have seen Sawako's post, realized that nothing had happened to her, and cringed at the memory of how scared she'd been, and how she'd set up this elaborate meeting.

Mai felt bad for Mayumi. So, because she figured Mayumi was probably mortified, Mai decided to break the ice.

It's Mai. Have you checked *Chain Mail* yet? Sawako's back!

Thank goodness nothing happened to her. When I think about the crazy way that we arranged to meet, I have to laugh. But when I was at the Internet café acting like a spy, I was really excited. It felt like I was doing something dangerous and important, and I don't think I've had that feeling before. So thank you for giving me such a great experience.

I feel like that kind of bonded us, even though we've never met. Why don't we e-mail each other sometimes outside of *Chain Mail?*

Mai sent the e-mail, then stood up. She hoped Mayumi would be less embarrassed once she realized that Mai had been equally silly, and that there were no hard feelings.

Mai hadn't realized how anxious she'd been until the tension had lifted. But she'd had a good time, maybe made a new friend, and everything was all right now. She didn't even feel too bad about missing the concert.

She went over to her stereo and pulled out her well-worn Black Thunder CD. Then she closed her eyes and let the music take her away.

MAYUMI

MONDAY, OCTOBER 13, 10:25 PM.

BEHIND NIHON JOSHI ACADEMY.

"Open your umbrella. You'll catch a cold."

Mayumi glanced up. Sayuri was standing in front of her under a red umbrella. She held out another umbrella to Mayumi.

"Thank you."

Mayumi had been in a daze for the last few hours, and didn't know when it had started raining. Her hair was plastered to her scalp, and stray tendrils dripped cold water down her face and neck.

"E-mail?" asked Sayuri.

For a moment Mayumi didn't know what she was talking about. Then she realized that she was still holding her cell phone. Raindrops ran down the screen. Mayumi wiped it with her damp sleeve.

"Yeah."

"A friend?"

"Kind of."

The girls fell silent. Mayumi was sitting on a seesaw, and it creaked as she shifted her weight. Sayuri's face looked very pale under the mercury streetlamps.

"How did you know I was here?" asked Mayumi.

Sayuri shrugged. "Intuition, I guess. We've been friends since elementary school, so I ought to know you by now. When I heard you hadn't gone home, I pretended I was you, and I ended up coming straight here."

"You called my house?"

"No, actually, the team captain did. When you didn't come back, everyone was worried, but Coach Nakazawa said you must have gone home. We finally called your house and when your mother said you weren't home, there was this huge panic." Sayuri snickered. "The person who was most panicked was Coach Nakazawa. He went completely white, and he started screaming, 'Everyone, get out and look for her! Go! Go! Go!' Serves him right."

"Oh." Mayumi should have been pleased, or at least amused, but she found that she no longer cared one way or another about Coach Nakazawa. She stood up. The rain darkened the pale wood where she had been sitting.

Sayuri offered Mayumi her hand. "Come on. Let's go back."

Mayumi didn't take Sayuri's outstretched hand. Instead, she touched Sayuri gently on the arm. "I'm quitting badminton."

Sayuri's hand twitched in surprise and raindrops bounced off her umbrella.

"Coach Nakazawa was right," said Mayumi. "He's a jerk, and it was a shock to me, but I've been sitting here thinking about it this whole time, and I've made my decision."

"But . . . but . . ." stammered Sayuri. "But what about me?"

"You'll be all right. You're only a freshman, but you're already beating juniors. Like Coach Nakazawa says, you've got the right stuff. You can handle Nihon Joshi without me—you belong here. I don't."

Sayuri stared at Mayumi like she'd gone out of her mind, but Mayumi kept talking. "I thought when I came in that it didn't matter what I did, as long as I was with you. I didn't think it would matter if I wasn't doing anything important to me, as long as you got a chance to shine. But it *does* matter. It matters to me."

The rain came down harder; the drops beat against the umbrellas like fingers on a drum. Mayumi raised her voice over the pounding rain. "It's like Coach Nakazawa said—everyone needs their own stage. Yours is on the badminton court. But mine is somewhere else."

"This is my fault!" blurted out Sayuri. "You see, you've gone through such a hard time because I forced Nihon Joshi to let you in. But, Mayumi, I thought it was what you wanted!"

"It was, back then," said Mayumi. "It just isn't any more. Don't be down on yourself, Sayuri. I've always known you got me in, and I'm glad. It's because of you that a klutz like me got six months on a star badminton team. And it's because of you that I realized what I really wanted."

"But I wanted to be together too," said Sayuri. "And now we won't be . . . and you've got new friends, right there!" She pointed to the cell phone. Then she looked down and said softly, "I'm sorry, this is so childish of me . . ."

"We'll still be the best of friends," Mayumi assured her. "Just not together all the time. Don't worry—now that I'm quitting the team, I have time for more than one friend. I'm quitting badminton, not *you.*"

Sayuri's eyes were huge and wet, as if she was about to cry. "Okay," she whispered.

"Don't look like that." Mayumi smiled. "I've been happy for you. Now you be happy for me. I think I've finally found what I was looking for."

The white light of the mercury lamp glinted off the cell phone that she held in her hand.

IV.

"Please understand that, right now, I am concealing something from you . . . I want you to know that there are things that I don't want you to know."

Roland Barthes
A Lover's Discourse: Fragments

MAI

TUESDAY, OCTOBER 14, 4:52 PM.

YOTSUYA, SUBDIVISION 3, MAI'S HOUSE.

Mayumi never wrote back. Mai guessed that she was too embarrassed. But still, she could have at least responded to one of the five e-mails Mai had sent her. Mai's relief at learning that Sawako was all right had faded into frustration with all the unresolved feelings and unanswered questions sparked by Sawako's four-day absence.

What had really happened to Sawako? Why hadn't Mayumi ever answered her e-mails? Where was Yukari?

Mai hurried toward her house. She had decided not to go out tonight, though the thought of inadvertently pleasing her mother by staying home annoyed her. But she was dying to catch Black Thunder's next show, and that was two thousand yen. If she went clubbing with her friends tonight, the cover charges and bus fare would be at least seven hundred yen. She had to stay in for a few nights to save up for that concert.

But she didn't mind spending a night at home in front of her computer. *Chain Mail* was going great. Sawako had written several more entries, and Mayumi had as well. Though she was unwilling to reply to Mai's e-mails, Mayumi had carefully replied to every single one of Sawako's entries. So far Sawako Shinoda had gotten the ride back to Tokyo and immediately contacted the police. Detective Murata had gone to the shack and found blood on the floor, but no other trace of Tsunoda.

The pace was quickening and Sawako's courage and Murata's righteous anger rose off the screen like smoke. *Chain Mail* was more gripping than any book Mai had ever read—not that she was a big reader.

The trouble was, there wasn't much room for Mai to participate. Sawako and Murata were working so closely together that *Chain Mail* had started to feel like their own private world. Worried that Kouhei might soon be forgotten entirely, Mai had posted an entry in which he began working with Murata as well.

And speaking of a world for two, Yukari also seemed to have been squeezed out. Sawako had hit Tsunoda in the face with a board and implied that he'd been seriously injured. For the sake of plausibility, he would have to take at least a few days to recover. It had been a great post, and probably Sawako hadn't thought that far ahead, but she'd really handicapped Yukari. Even if Yukari had returned from wherever she'd gone, it would be hard for her to come into the story right now.

But Mai was sure that Yukari was planning something. She'd been so wonderfully scary and inventively cruel up to this point that Mai couldn't imagine her defeated by a mere blow to the eyes. She was probably biding her time until Tsunoda made an unimaginably terrifying reappearance. *I'd better make sure I keep up.*

Clouds loomed low and gray above her, but Mai's mood brightened as she imagined what she could write tonight. Perhaps Kouhei could secretly meet Sawako to commiserate.

"I'm home," called Mai as she walked inside. There were two pairs of men's black leather shoes lined up at the entrance, and the living room door was open. Mai peered at the shoes, wondering if her father had invited a friend over. That was odd, because normally he wouldn't be home this early.

Her mother came out of the living room. "Mai—"

"We have guests?"

Her mother nodded. Her face was pale and the skin around her cheeks was stretched tight. "The police are here."

A shock went through Mai's body. She realized that her mother's expression was not merely worried, but suspicious: she thought the police were after Mai!

She doesn't trust me.

But I know I haven't done anything illegal. So what can they want?

Her mother seemed to have to force words out of her mouth. "Mai . . . You haven't done anything wrong, have you?"

Disgusted, Mai ignored her and went straight into the living room.

The policemen were both wearing black suits and sitting with their backs to the door. They turned, then stood up when she came in. One was a young man who parted his hair in the middle, and the other was a middle-aged man whose hair had prematurely grayed.

The older man spoke first. "You're Mai Kishimoto, right? We're sorry to bother you. I'm sure you've had a long day at school."

Get to the point! Mai wanted to shriek, but managed to restrain herself.

"I'm Detective Shiota from the Juveniles Division of the Shibuya precinct." The white-haired detective smiled as he offered her his card. "And this is Detective Yamazaki, also from Shibuya."

The young cop held out his business card as well, but he didn't smile. "I'm Yamazaki."

"I haven't done anything!" Mai blurted out.

Detective Shiota looked startled. He glanced at Mai and her mother, who were standing side by side; Mai clutched her schoolbag and her mother clenched her hands into fists.

"Oh, no, it's nothing like that!" Detective Shiota exclaimed. "I'm so sorry—I did it again. I should have explained to your mother why we're here. Man, the chief is always yelling at me for stuff like this."

Mai began to relax. This blundering cop was nothing like the formidable Detective Murata. She wasn't afraid of him any more. "Do you need me for something?" she snapped.

"Mai!" said her mother. "Don't be rude!"

"It's all right," said Detective Shiota. "It's my fault. Don't worry, Mai, you didn't do anything wrong. We're just here to check a few things with you about an incident we had recently."

"An incident?" echoed Mai.

Detective Shiota gestured at the sofa. "Please, have a seat. This will just take a moment, and then we'll be out of here."

Once Mai sat down, Detective Shiota spoke calmly, "Do you know about the case where a junior high freshman girl disappeared?"

Mai's heart began to pound. The palms of her hands tingled as she started to sweat. *Stay calm!* She ordered herself. *If you panic, they'll suspect you.*

"Oh, yes," she said, and was relieved to hear that her voice didn't shake. "I saw it on TV."

"I see. Did you know that the case has been solved?"

"What? No." Once Sawako had returned, Mai had lost interest in the "missing girl" case. But if it had been solved, then why were the police questioning her about it?

"You know, the media loves reporting on a story while it's hot, but they've got a short attention span. If it turns out that there's no scandal or no one's dead, they lose interest. When it was 'police are baffled by missing girl case,' it was front-page news." Detective Shiota sighed. "Like I said, the case has been solved. But there's one aspect that's still a bit troublesome."

"What do you mean, 'troublesome'?"

The detective paused. "Mai, you haven't received any unusual e-mails lately, have you?"

" 'Unusual'?" Mai bit her tongue, embarrassed to echo the detective again. But he was so vague! "You mean, like spam or online dating schemes?"

Detective Shiota shook his head. "No, not spam. Mail from someone named Sawako."

Mai tried not to choke. But she couldn't prevent her mind from racing.

So Sawako was kidnapped, after all! But then why did she go back to Chain Mail *like nothing happened? And why do the police know about me? I've never met Sawako, so how did they find me? They must have found* Chain Mail! *That's where they got my e-mail address, and I guess they managed to trace my home address from that.*

Detective Shiota's somber eyes gazed steadily at Mai. "Is something the matter, Mai?"

He's not stupid at all . . . That was a trick to make me let down my guard. He must know everything already, and he just wants me to admit it. But I haven't done anything wrong . . .

"Mai?" repeated Detective Shiota. "You did get an e-mail from Sawako, didn't you?"

Mai nodded.

"When was that?"

"I think around the beginning of October."

"Around the third?" His voice was gentle, but he wasn't bothering with the "bumbling detective" routine any more.

"Probably. I don't really remember."

"And what did you do?"

"With the e-mail?"

"Did you write a response?"

Mai had only a second to make her decision, before he noticed her hesitation. "I deleted it."

"Why?"

"Well . . ." Mai glanced at the younger detective, but he was watching her even more intently than Detective Shiota. She turned back to the older man. "Well, it was from a stranger, so it seemed kind of creepy. I mean, I didn't pay that much attention to it. I get lots of spam, and I just automatically delete it."

"What did it say?" Detective Yamazaki asked suddenly. Mai twitched nervously at the sharpness of his tone.

"She asked me to be her pen-pal, I think. I didn't read it that closely."

Detective Yamazaki jotted this down without even a nod to acknowledge her response.

"Is that all?" inquired Detective Shiota. "Did she say anything else?"

The detectives were firing off their questions quickly, as if they were trying to stop Mai from taking any time to think about her responses.

"I don't remember," she said. That seemed like the safest response.

"But you definitely got an e-mail from Sawako?"

"Yes."

The detectives glanced at each other.

Mai's mother suddenly spoke. She had been standing behind the sofa and had been so quiet that Mai had forgotten she was in the room. "Can I ask what this is all about?"

Detective Shiota plastered on a fake smile when he addressed her. "Yes. I barged into your house and questioned your daughter, so I think you both deserve to know what's going on. So I'll tell you what happened, but since all the parties involved are minors, I can't tell you their names." He paused.

"You heard about the girl who disappeared. That wasn't exactly the type of kidnapping that the media claimed it was. That is, a girl—I'll just call her 'the victim'—*was* held against her will, but it wasn't by an adult. It was two other teenage girls. One was a junior from the victim's junior high school, and the other was a high school freshman. They did hold her hostage, but it wasn't quite as sinister a situation as we'd thought at first. The older girls did it because they were angry at the victim—she'd pulled a sort of prank on them and they decided to pull one on her. It seems that the victim had stolen e-mail addresses from the junior's cell phone . . ."

Detective Shiota gazed at Mai as if he could read her mind, and she swallowed guiltily. He seemed to take note of that, then continued his story.

"At the beginning of April, a hundred teenage girls in Tokyo all received an unusual e-mail from someone who called herself Sawako, asking if they'd like to write a story with her. Most of the girls thought it was spam or just weren't interested and they ignored it. But about a dozen of them didn't. Those girls were all friends with the junior who was the queen bee of a clique of tough girls. It didn't seem to be the normal kind of spam, so they thought it was odd that they'd all gotten it at the same time.

"Those girls compared notes, and they figured out that the junior was the only one who had all of their e-mail addresses. But she denied sending the Sawako e-mail, and her friends thought it didn't seem like something she'd do. So they wondered—who was Sawako and how had she gotten their addresses? They tried replying to the original e-mail, but Sawako never wrote back. That just made them even more curious."

The detective sighed. "The girls were quick to figure out what had happened. In just two days, they began to suspect the victim. She was a freshman girl who went to the same school as the junior, and supposedly she'd had the junior's cell phone for a while. I say 'supposedly' because the victim denied it. But there was circumstantial evidence to suggest that she had taken that cell phone for a few hours. The junior had accidentally left her phone in the bathroom while the victim was there. The junior realized it was missing and returned for it, but by then both the victim and the phone were gone. Later that day, another girl found the phone in the bathroom and returned it to the junior.

So the girls in the clique came to the conclusion that the victim must have stolen their friend's phone, spent some time downloading its address book into her own phone, and then put it back where she'd found it."

Mai was having a hard time keeping the story straight. "So the freshman—the victim—took the junior's phone, went into its address book, and typed all the e-mail addresses in it into her own cell phone?"

Detective Yamazaki answered her. "No, she wouldn't have needed to type them out. We think she connected the junior's cell phone to a computer, downloaded the addresses, and then connected her own phone to the computer and uploaded them into her own address book. The school has a computer room, and we determined that it's possible to do that on their computers."

Mai had occasionally peeked at other girls' address books to see who their friends were, but she was amazed that anyone would go so far as to secretly acquire someone else's address book. "Are you sure that's what happened? Did she say she did it? Did she say why?"

"No, the victim denied that she ever took the junior's cell phone," said Detective Yamazaki. "We checked the victim's cell phone and there was no stolen data on it. But she could have deleted it. And there is a record of her having entered the computer room, so we believe that—"

Detective Shiota poked Detective Yamazaki with his elbow. Detective Yamazaki snapped his mouth closed.

Detective Shiota put on the genial smile that Mai found more and more alarming as the interview went on. "We don't know for sure what happened with the two girls and their cell phones. But the important thing is that the junior and her friends thought that the victim had taken private information that belonged to the junior. So a high school boy who was a friend of the junior's waylaid the victim and grilled her for information. When she wouldn't confess, he refused to let her go home."

"Wait, wait," said Mai's mother. "Was Mai's e-mail address one of the addresses on the junior's cell phone?"

"That's right."

"Oh no!" cried Mai's mother, and covered her face with her hands. "You think Mai was involved in the kidnapping?!"

Mai looked away in disgust. *She pretends to be so trusting. But instead of defending me, she jumps to the conclusion that I was involved.*

"No, ma'am," said Detective Shiota hastily. He directed a sympathetic look at Mai's mother, then at Mai, as if he sensed trouble and was trying to diffuse the tension between them. "Your daughter is not a suspect. We're only gathering evidence about the chain of events that led to the victim being abducted for four days. We need to confirm or disprove the story about the cell phone, since that seems to be the crux of events. So we're talking to all the girls in the junior's address book to ask if they got an e-mail from 'Sawako,' and what it said."

Detective Shiota held Mai's gaze. She realized that he knew that she'd lied, and she felt hurt and ashamed. But she couldn't bear to expose the private world of *Chain Mail* to the probing questions and prying eyes of the detectives—or worse, to her mother.

"Anyway, thank you for your cooperation," said Detective Shiota. "That's all we needed to know. I don't think we'll be back to bother you again."

Detective Shiota nodded to the younger man, and they both stood up.

"Who was it?" demanded Mai. "Who was the junior who had my e-mail address?"

Both men stopped at the sharpness of her tone. Then they turned toward her with the offhand curiosity of well-fed cats eyeing a mouse that they've already decided wasn't worth the chase.

Mai broke their gaze and stared at the table in front of her instead. She was furious with her mother for pretending to trust her and revealing that she didn't, and with the detectives for pretending to be kind when really they just couldn't be bothered with exposing the lies that they knew she'd told.

"I'm afraid we can't tell you that," said Detective Shiota, with no trace of alarm or interest in his voice. "In cases involving minors, the identity of both victims and perpetrators is always kept secret."

"But she has my e-mail address!" said Mai. "It has to be someone I know, so why not tell me who it is?"

Detective Shiota gave her an apologetic smile. "That's true, you probably do know her. But we don't think your connection to her is deep enough to warrant revealing her identity. You didn't get an e-mail from a junior asking if you'd gotten an e-mail from Sawako, did you?"

"No."

"The junior had about a hundred addresses on her cell phone. But she only discussed the Sawako e-mail with ten or twelve of her friends. So you and the other eighty people she didn't mention it to are probably acquaintances of hers, not close friends."

"Then please tell me the name of the girl she kidnapped," begged Mai. "I might know this Sawako girl. Maybe I know something that could help your investigation."

Detective Shiota's eyes narrowed and it seemed to Mai that he was seriously considering her offer. But then he shook his head. "I'm sorry, but I can't tell you that either. We believe that your relationship to both the victim and the perpetrator is peripheral, at most. After all, you deleted that e-mail without even reading the whole thing, right? So you don't have much of a connection with this affair. Right?"

Her mother already thought Mai might have helped kidnap someone. If Mai confessed to lying to the police, it would cement her mother's lack of faith in her and drag *Chain Mail* out into the withering light of day.

Slowly, Mai nodded. "Right."

"By the way, you shouldn't give out your e-mail address to people that you don't know very well. You wouldn't give out your home phone number to some stranger, would you? You should think about your e-mail and cell phone number the same way. You have no way of knowing who might misuse your personal information. A lot of stalking cases have begun over e-mail. So please be careful."

Mai ground her teeth.

Her mother answered for her. "I'll make sure that she is."

Mai's mother followed the detectives out of the living room, bowing the entire way. They paused in the entry way for the police to put on their shoes. Once they were out of the room, Mai couldn't hear them clearly, but she picked up enough of their conversation to know that they were still discussing the case. Mai would have eavesdropped, but the sound of Detective Shiota's "sorry ma'am" and "confidential" convinced her that her mother wasn't getting any more information out of him than Mai had.

So Sawako was kidnapped, thought Mai. *Not by a stalker, but by teenagers who were mad at her for stealing some girl's address book. But why did Sawako steal the addresses in the first place?*

Mai thought back to the original e-mail she had gotten from Sawako.

Hi, I'm Sawako. I'm a girl (obviously) and a first year student at a private junior high school in Tokyo. I got this e-mail, and it seemed interesting—really, it's not a boring spam message—so I'm forwarding it to you.

Sawako had wanted other people to participate in *Chain Mail*. When Mai had gotten the message, there was still one role available. Sawako must have had trouble finding the last person. Maybe she'd already sent it to everyone she knew, and not enough of them had responded. So she had stolen the junior's cell phone to get access to the popular girl's network of friends.

She wanted the fictional world so badly . . . Mai felt as if a hand had closed over her heart and squeezed tightly.

Sawako must not have had many friends, if she needed to borrow someone else's acquaintances to find just one more girl. Maybe she was shy or bad at small talk, but whatever the reason was, she must have a hard time dealing with people in the real world.

But she loves stories and she's a very good writer. So even if at first she tried talking to people over e-mail, she probably got sick of one-line e-mails and people who write things like "LOL" and "XD" and "Gackt is teh SMEX, squee!" She must have wanted something more serious and in-depth. So when she got the message from Yukari, she must have thought that Chain Mail *was the perfect way to connect with other girls who wanted to write stories.*

For the first time, Mai felt like she really knew Sawako, the author, as opposed to her character, Sawako Shinoda. She felt so much compassion for Sawako that it hurt deep inside.

What could it have been like for her, to be dragged away and held prisoner, far away from her home and her beloved Chain Mail? *She must have been terrified.*

When Mai had read that post about Sawako Shinoda being kidnapped by Tsunoda, she had been both thrilled by the story and relieved that the author was all right after all. She had never imagined that something bad *had* happened to her, and that Sawako had used it for inspiration. When Mai imagined Sawako sitting in front of her computer or cell phone, taking a traumatic experience and transforming it into a part of the story they loved, tears came to Mai's eyes.

I want to meet her, she thought. *I want to meet her and tell her it's okay.* Mai was surprised by how close she felt to Sawako. Somehow Sawako had become important to Mai; not just a pen-pal, but a real friend.

"Mai, please don't make me worry about you." Her mother stalked into the room. Her face did not display the expression of a cool, hip, with-it mother who was well versed in American child psychology, but that of a normal, hysterical mother.

Mai was annoyed at this interruption. "None of this had anything to do with me. The police said so themselves."

"I know you didn't do anything personally, but you need to be more selective about who you hang out with. Some girl who has your e-mail address is a criminal!"

"Look, I don't even know who that is. Anyway, it's not my responsibility if someone I barely know kidnaps someone I probably don't know at all."

"No, but it's your responsibility not to associate with gang girls and kidnappers!"

"So what am I supposed to do? Make people sign an oath that they won't kidnap anyone before I say hello to them?"

Mai's mother glared at her daughter. "Don't you scowl at me like that, young lady. The reason I've let you have so much freedom is that I trusted you to make wise choices. I've let you run around after dark, dressing in weird outfits and going to concerts, because I thought you knew that clubs were fun, but school was what was important for your future. Well, it looks like I was wrong."

As her mother continued to speak, Mai noticed that her flapping pink lips enclosed a pit of darkness. It reminded her of an effect at a Black Thunder concert, where the petals of a huge red rose withered and fell away, and revealed the worm-like monster that had been devouring it from within.

What if that woman blabbering at me was just a shell? What if that darkness inside her mouth was the entrance to the cavern where my mother's true form resides? What sort of creature would lurk inside that wet red tunnel?

Maybe something with scales—waxy ones, so the saliva and mucus would slide off it . . . A hideous worm-snake inside a slimy abyss.

Mai shuddered at the thought. Then she steeled herself, and let her imagination wander where it pleased.

Meanwhile, the mother-creature kept ranting. "No matter how good you are, if you hang out with a bad crowd, their reputation will rub off on you. And you never know—even if you mean well, you can still get pulled into going along with whatever the people around you are doing."

The mother-creature's mouth split open at the corners. With a sound like paper tearing, her cheeks began to rip apart. "I believe you when you say you don't know anything about the kidnapping. But still—"

Her jaw rotated upward until it pointed at the ceiling, then her entire head blew apart. Two bloodshot eyes thrust up from the ruined skull, rotating slowly on pallid stalks. "It obviously isn't a good idea for a junior high girl like you to go to clubs."

"What?!" cried out Mai. She was so upset at her mother, and repulsed by the mother-creature, that she had to turn away and speak to the wall. "What do clubs have to do with this? Why are you blaming my music? This is so stupid!"

"Mai! Don't you dare call me stupid. Listen, I'm saying this because I'm worried about you . . ."

Mai heard footsteps as something—her mother, or the mother-creature—approached her. "Get away from me!"

Mai ran out of the living room, taking care not to look back. She slammed the hallway door, then dashed upstairs. Once she was in her room, she locked the door.

"Don't come in here!" she yelled through the door. Then she leaned back against the door and locked her arms over her face.

She knew that the mother-creature had just been a fantasy, albeit a vivid and disturbing one. But she still didn't want to let her mother into her room—or into *Chain Mail's* world.

And it wasn't only her mother. She wanted to keep the police, teachers, and even her friends out as well. It was a private world that was only big enough for four. If too many people got in, they'd tear it apart.

There were people who believed that there was only one world, the one they woke up to every day. They had no imagination, nor the courage to let it take them wherever it might lead. There were people who only wanted one world, or wouldn't admit it if they wanted more. They spent all their time in their everyday lives, even if that meant they never got a chance to shine.

There were people who did their best to be exactly like everybody else.

There were people who harassed anyone who was different, making them isolated and unwanted.

Mai couldn't deal with those kinds of people. She believed that there was an infinite number of worlds.

She was drawn to people who, though they had only one body, had several personas. Like Black Thunder. The members of the band all had part-time jobs, sweating in road construction or pouring drinks at a pub. While they worked, they lived in the same world as the detectives and Mai's mother. But when they got on stage, they had different faces. They were radiant.

Sawako is the one who showed me where I could shine.

"It's all right," Mai murmured aloud. "I protected us. I lied to the detectives to protect our world."

The sun had set and the sky had changed from crimson to a deep indigo. She hadn't turned on the lights, so her room was dark and cold.

"Sawako, I want to meet you," she whispered. She put her hand in her pocket and took out her cell phone. Mai opened it and pulled up the e-mail Sawako had sent her.

Hi, I'm Sawako. I'm a girl (obviously) and a first year student at a private junior high school in Tokyo.

The reply button was at the bottom of the screen.

If I hit that button, I can connect with Sawako. But should I? Her finger wavered.

DATE AND TIME: OCTOBER 15, 3:10 PM
AUTHOR: MAYUMI
CHARACTER: DETECTIVE MURATA

Tsunoda disappeared again. We staked out his house, but he never returned. He didn't send any more nasty little packages, either. Though Sawako had injured him, it hadn't been serious enough to force him to go to a hospital. He was probably lurking somewhere off the beaten path, licking his wounds for a while before he made his next move. Now would be the perfect time to nab him—except we had no idea where he was.

The local police at the Mishima precinct had combed the hills around Kannami town, where Sawako had turned up. They used dogs and helicopters, but found nothing but an empty shack and some blood on the floor.

The detective in Mishima sounded defensive when I called him. "You can't expect one search in the hills to turn up the suspect," he said. "People get lost for days out there. It's only been twelve hours since the victim was found, and the roads in those hills lead out in all directions. You can walk all the way to Atami. If you cross the mountains in the other direction, you can get to Numazu. And it wouldn't even take twelve hours to get to Mishima city. We're doing our best, but we've got a huge area to cover."

"Well, keep searching," I insisted. "This is a very serious matter. The victim is terrified, and with good reason. She's afraid to go to school. As long as Tsunoda is out there, she won't feel safe anywhere."

DATE AND TIME: OCTOBER 15, 3:57 PM
AUTHOR: SAWAKO
CHARACTER: SAWAKO SHINODA

I didn't leave my house today.

When I lie in my bed at night, I remember opening my eyes in the shack, where it was so dark that I thought I'd gone blind. I can't bear to turn out the lights when I try to sleep. Just closing my eyes is traumatic.

When I do doze off, I dream that I'm back there. And then I wake up, afraid to try to sleep again. Then it's morning, and I'm more exhausted than I was the night before.

Mama quit her wine-tasting class at the culture school so she could stay with me. Newspaper and television reporters keep coming around, asking for interviews. But the more they insist, the more I wonder if I want to speak out or if I'd rather stay hidden. They want me to be the heroine of this horror story, and explain the true danger of stalkers to an ignorant public. But how can I be a heroine when I get the shakes every time the doorbell rings?

When I open the front door, a crack and the light shines in . . . I get so scared that I have to slam it. I worry that *he's* hiding outside, inside, in the closet, under the bed, behind the shower curtain, on the roof. I'm afraid to check, but I'm afraid not to check.

I can't go on like this.

MAYUMI

WEDNESDAY, OCTOBER 15, 4:12 PM.

SEIBU SHINJUKU LINE—A LOCAL TRAIN BOUND FOR KAMISHAKUJI.

As Mayumi finished reading the latest post on her cell phone, she got the feeling that someone was watching her. She glanced around the train. No one was looking at her, nor did anyone quickly turn away if their eyes did meet.

She peered out the window. It was a little after four in the afternoon, which made it the first time she'd headed home this early since she'd started junior high. It was a local train, too, which gave it an even more relaxed feeling. Every seat was occupied, but only a few people stood up. There were a couple of old ladies with shopping bags and one sleepy businessman, but most of the car was occupied by junior high and high school students.

Mayumi amused herself by studying everyone's school uniforms. A girl across from her wore the exclusive Shouei Girls' School uniform, which meant she was smart. The girl next to her was in the Shinagawa Girls' School uniform, which was much cuter than Mayumi's. A lively group of girls in white sailor uniforms had gotten in at Araiyakushi-mae station and were sitting together in the back of the car.

One girl stood near the door. She was reading a paperback book, and her hair fell down over her bent head, covering her face. Although Mayumi couldn't see her well, she guessed the girl was also a junior high freshman. She seemed withdrawn. As if to match her dark demeanor, her uniform was navy blue and very plain. It was more of a regular outfit than a real uniform, in fact—there was no emblem on the blazer, and only a paltry three pleats in the knee-length skirt. She probably went to a public school.

At least my uniform's better than that, thought Mayumi. *I really am glad I go to a private school.* She smiled and stretched out in her seat, though not so much as to sprawl over anyone else. It had been so long since she'd been able to relax like this. When she'd been on the badminton team, she'd never had a day off. They didn't even keep a lighter schedule during exam weeks. She was always exhausted when she dragged her heavy racket case aboard the packed express train.

But she had thought that was normal. She thought that was just how it was for the members of the badminton team, and that being a member was merely her fate. More than that: she'd thought that being a team member was the *only* thing she could be.

It was something she'd started believing on her own. She had pushed herself into that miserable life and told herself it was the only choice there was. If she'd just been honest with herself earlier, she could have enjoyed this local train, this relaxed little world, much sooner.

She had been so worried about so many things. She had let her imagination run away with her to the point of setting up a meeting with Mai to discuss Sawako. But then she'd been so upset over losing her place on the badminton team that she didn't even reply to Mai's e-mails. By the time she'd composed herself, she saw a brief article in the paper saying that the missing girl was back and it had all been some kind of misunderstanding—so that girl couldn't have been Sawako, after all.

Mayumi did plan to respond to Mai's final e-mail, the one asking to be pen-pals outside of *Chain Mail*, but not just yet. It seemed like *Chain Mail* was building up to a climax, and since there was no real-life crisis, Mayumi preferred to keep her worlds separate. When the story was concluded, she'd write to Mai. And then maybe they'd start a new story, but it would be different, because then they'd know each other in real life too. (But *this* story was special because, not knowing the people behind the characters, it seemed so real. It would be a shame to change that before the end.) Once *Chain Mail* was over, she'd e-mail Mai and explain why she hadn't written earlier. She was sure Mai would understand.

This is my stage, thought Mayumi. *I'm not going to do anything that might mess with my perfect little world.*

With Sawako Shinoda traumatized and hiding at home, Kouhei pushed off to the sidelines, and Tsunoda forced to spend time recuperating offstage, Detective Murata had become the main character. *It's all up to me to keep the story moving.*

Mayumi scratched her head as she pondered Murata's next move. Then she got that strange feeling again.

Someone is definitely watching me.

This time she kept her face lowered, but discreetly glanced around the train. There was the sleepy businessman, a housewife who was glaring out the window and clutching a shopping bag, and the girl from Shinagawa Girls' School, who was writing in a workbook. None of them seemed to be paying any attention to Mayumi.

A young man was sitting in the seat farthest away from Mayumi, next to the public school girl. He looked about twenty years old, and wore a plain white T-shirt and dingy jeans. He was a bit chubby, with plump fingers and a round face. His skin was pale, and his silver-rimmed glasses were smudgy.

Could it be that guy?

He wasn't looking at her now. He was flipping through a magazine, his thick lips pursed as if he disapproved of his own reading material. But he could have noticed that she was looking around the train and immediately started pretending to read.

He looks kind of like Tsunoda, thought Mayumi. *That's creepy.*

Tsunoda wasn't chubby and his glasses had black rims, not silver ones. But the man on the subway also had grubby clothes and glasses that needed cleaning. Tsunoda's hair was described as long and greasy, which was close enough to the man's shoulder-length cut. And like the stalker, his cheeks and chin were covered with mangy stubble.

Once Mayumi had made the connection between them, she couldn't get it out of her head.

"The next stop, Kamishakujii, is the final stop for this train. Passengers heading for Musashiseki and Kodaira, please exit and wait for the next train."

Mayumi took the conductor's announcement as her cue to stand up. The man glanced at her. *He was looking at me!* she thought.

She hurried out of the train as soon as the doors opened. The businessman, the housewives, and the girls in sailor suits left the train in one big mob, heading for the stairs that led outside.

Mayumi stayed on the platform to wait for the next train. The public school girl got off the train and stood behind her. Then the young man with the silver rimmed glasses stepped up to wait behind that girl.

Mayumi was alarmed. *Could he really be a stalker? But why follow me? Maybe he's a pedophile. But there were plenty of other girls on the train. I'll get away from him, just to be on the safe side.*

She began to walk along the platform as quickly as she could while still trying to look nonchalant. If she ran, that would only draw his attention. She trotted along, resisting the urge to look back during the excruciatingly long time it took before she reached the platform.

When she got there, she nervously turned to see if the man had followed her.

He hadn't. But the public school girl had. Or, at least, she was there, standing in the shadow of a pillar.

Mayumi sighed in relief. Her heart was still pounding. *Maybe she thought that guy was weird, too. Well, I'm glad we're both all right.*

She flipped open her cell phone, eager to write the next part.

MAI

FRIDAY, OCTOBER 17, 4:35 PM.

SHIBUYA, NEW YORKER'S CAFÉ.

When Mai called to find out where they were meeting, she was given an extremely complicated set of directions.

"You know Central Street, right? Go straight down, until you come to a McDonald's. Turn right there. Keep walking until you come to a big street with an ABC Mart, then take the narrow path next to that. You'll pass a Murasaki Sports store, and then the street starts running uphill—that's called Spain Hill. So go up that . . ."

In New York City, directions usually consisted of an address and the subway stop; in Tokyo they had to be long and detailed. But as Mai listened to the other girl talk, she gradually realized that all the paths were ones she'd taken before. Every teenager in Tokyo knew how to get to Spain Hill—it was a hugely popular hang-out spot. Mai wondered if the other girl was making fun of her.

"Meet me at the New Yorker's Café. If you can't find it, ask around. I'll be there until about five. That is, if I go there tomorrow. Sometimes I don't go, so if I'm not there, sorry."

The girl on the other end of the phone was Yuki Kanai, a junior from Kioi Academy (one of the top three girls' junior high schools).

She had a reputation for being a bit of a bad girl. She was also the one who had kidnapped Sawako.

Mai really wanted to meet Sawako, or at least exchange an e-mail or phone call. She had tried to dig up Sawako's phone number, but no one seemed to have it.

Mai couldn't understand exactly how it was that she'd come to feel so close to a girl she'd never met, but she was convinced that if she didn't manage to connect with Sawako, she would come to regret it.

But if Mai e-mailed Sawako a message saying, "Sawako, are you all right? I'm worried about you," it would go against the unspoken rules of *Chain Mail*. If Mai wrote, "I lied to two policemen to protect our world," it would sound pathetic and creepy.

And she knew what Sawako might think: "We shouldn't meet face-to-face. We shouldn't gossip about our boyfriends, squeal over bands we like, repeat rumors about our friends, or complain about our parents. That's what the real world is for. *Chain Mail* is special because it's not about those trivial everyday things."

If Mai couldn't meet Sawako, then at the very least she wanted to meet the girl who had *kidnapped* Sawako. Sneaking around like this was horrible, but Yuki was the only one who could provide information about Sawako. And if Mai knew exactly what had happened to Sawako, it would give her a better idea of who Sawako was and what she might be going through now.

It took Mai two days to get Yuki's e-mail address. She had called everyone she knew, from her classmates to girls she had met in clubs.

They were surprised to get a call from her, because Mai wasn't especially close to any of them, and rarely spoke on the phone. And when Mai explained that she had called to ask if they knew anything about the girl who had been kidnapped, several of them were freaked out, and one of them actually hung up on her.

The girls she knew from clubs were even less helpful. Mai had snubbed most of them for being groupies who tried to meet their favorite stars in person. Even if she hadn't come right out and said so, they had all apparently noticed her attitude. When she called with such an odd question, they were cold and hostile.

Mai realized that her lack of interest in spending time with other teenagers had shielded her from realizing just how badly she was coming across. It was clear that nobody liked her, and the worst part was that she knew exactly why. She wished she had been a nicer person, and not just because being more likable would make it a lot easier to get in touch with Sawako.

The only girl who was willing to talk to her was one she barely knew. That girl was a club acquaintance, but one whose musical tastes didn't overlap much with Mai's, so they hardly ever went to the same shows. Because of that, the girl hadn't caught the sharp edge of Mai's sarcastic tongue, and to Mai's relief, she'd been friendly when she took Mai's call.

"I know what you're talking about," said the girl casually. "I got that e-mail from Sawako too. The girl you want to talk to is Yuki Kanai." She gave Mai the phone number.

Mai vaguely recalled Yuki Kanai. About a year and a half ago, before she had discovered Black Thunder, Mai had gone to a club in Ichikawa to see a J-rock band. That night the club was doing a weird mixed set, with pop bands, J-rock bands, and even a cyber-trance DJ. Yuki had come to the club to hear the DJ, but had stayed for the whole set. It had been a small club, and she and Mai had stood next to each other and talked about music.

Mai guessed she had managed not to insult Yuki, because the girls had exchanged phone numbers and e-mail addresses. But they had never contacted each other, and when Mai had gotten a new cell phone, she hadn't bothered to transfer Yuki's information. But Yuki must have kept Mai's, and that was how Sawako had been able to e-mail Mai.

Mai telephoned Yuki, and Yuki had suggested that they meet up in Shibuya.

Though Mai knew Spain Hill well, she had never been to the New Yorker Café, so she carefully followed Yuki's directions.

Hey, it's behind Parco Part 2, Mai realized. She had been to that place several times, because she had furnished her room with a desk, chair, and clock from a store called Franc Franc. If she had realized that was where the café was, she could have avoided the crowded areas of Central Street and Spain Hill, and instead cut through the park. It would have been faster that way and she wouldn't have gotten caught in a downpour.

Irritated, Mai shoved her umbrella into the café's umbrella stand.

"Welcome!" the clerk greeted her from behind the counter.

Mai nodded and looked around for Yuki. The café was a lot bigger than she had expected, with a smoking section to the right and a non-smoking section to the left. She spotted four tough-looking girls on the far side of the smoking section, all puffing away under a haze of gray smoke. She headed straight for them.

One of them looked up. "Mai Kishimoto?"

"Yuki Kanai?"

The girl nodded. She was the tallest of the bunch. She wore a tight pink tank top, a tighter denim mini-skirt, and Nike sneakers. Her bare legs were crossed. "These are my accomplices," said Yuki. "Saki, Akemi, and Tomoko."

Mai was taken aback by how casually Yuki used the word "accomplices." She gave them a brief nod.

Even though it was halfway through October and raining, the girls wore either camisoles or thin T-shirts. They looked Mai over from head to toe. She immediately felt self-conscious about having come straight over from school without bothering to change out of her uniform.

Yuki stuck her cigarette between her shiny pink lips and took a long drag. "Go buy something."

Unnerved, Mai went and got a cup of coffee. When she returned with it, Yuki's friends gave her the same stares all over again.

Yuki looked into Mai's cup. Her dyed-brown bangs fell into her eyebrows. "What did you get?"

"The house blend. Tall."

"Lame!" The girl with black hair, Akemi, laughed like she was the only one in the world who knew what was funny.

Tomoko, the girl in parachute pants, joined in a moment later.

Yuki sliced her hand through the air in a "cut it" gesture. "Mai's a real New Yorker, not just a Tokyo girl in a New Yorker café. They don't drink girly things like caramel macchiatos over there."

Mai wondered how Yuki knew she had lived in New York. Had she mentioned it when they had met in Ichikawa? Or had Yuki researched her after Mai had called?

Yuki glanced at Mai's gray skirt. "That's the Shirogane Preparatory uniform. You must be smart."

"You're from Kioi Academy," replied Mai. "You must be smarter."

Yuki snorted.

"Not any more," said Saki. "They just cut her."

"They cut all of us," said Tomoko. "It sucks."

Saki rolled her blue-shadowed eyes. She and Yuki laughed.

Mai didn't. "Did you drop out?"

"I was forced to," said Yuki, still keeping a fake smile on her face. "We were all going to private schools, but they don't tolerate scandal. So when the police started investigating us, the schools couldn't kick us out fast enough."

Tomoko flipped back her shaggy chestnut hair and grinned. "It was different for Yuki, though. It was easy for them to let us go—our grades were marginal anyway. But Yuki was a star student."

Akemi added, "Our schools were really hung up on how low our test scores were. So when we got involved in a police matter, that was all they needed. They told me that if people found out that they were keeping students who had scored so low, it would affect their applications for the next year. So that was that." She inspected a lock of her hair, then bit off a split end.

Yuki said, "Officially, we're transferring, because you can't get expelled from junior high."

"The official word is 'cut,' isn't it?" said Saki cheerfully.

Mai was amazed that the girls could laugh about being in trouble with the police and getting expelled. Or were they putting on a brave front to cover their real feelings?

"Um, about Sawako . . ." said Mai nervously.

Yuki's smile vanished and she gave Mai a sharp look. "Why do you want to know about her?"

"Well, I got an e-mail from her. I guess it seemed weird to me that I was connected to someone who was involved in a big news story."

Yuki sighed. "I wouldn't get too involved with her, if I was you. This started out as a tiny little prank and it got blown up into a big deal. I have a feeling that anyone who gets close to her could get caught up in some heavy stuff, and I don't want it to be you. And I *really* don't want it to be me again."

Mai was surprised by Yuki's advice. Even though Mai had come this far already, she was still afraid to tell Yuki the whole story. Yuki and her friends were all smoking illegally, they laughed about getting expelled, and their whole demeanor made Mai realize that compared to these bad girls, her own tough front was nothing more than a transparent pose.

These girls had actually kidnapped someone and didn't even deny it, but brazenly called each other "accomplices."

And yet Yuki's advice had sounded sincere and well intended. She seemed concerned about her friends and even about Mai, whom she barely knew.

I don't think Yuki's a bad person, thought Mai. Though they hadn't spoken for more than five minutes, Mai had a good feeling about her. *There has to be more to the kidnapping than this.*

As if answering Mai's thought, Yuki sighed again. "She came on her own." The other girls, who had been laughing up until now, quickly fell silent.

"I only wanted to scare her," explained Yuki. "I was pissed off at her for stealing my friends' addresses and sending them weird messages. Besides, I was supposed to be this big tough girl and she was a thirteen-year-old nobody. I felt like I had to do something, or everyone would think I was a wimp.

"I got my friends here together and we followed Sawako after school. Once she wasn't around any other students, we went up to her and told her she had to come with us to Shibuya. But we thought the four of us weren't scary enough, so we called in some boys to back us up. Some of them were our boyfriends and some of them were just guys we hung out with, but they were all from high school and junior high.

"We all sat down at a café together. We confronted her about the e-mails, but she was stubborn. No matter what we said, she wouldn't admit that she had stolen my cell phone. Finally, I figured we'd probably scared her enough, so we ditched her and went to a club. But halfway through the set, I happened to look across the room, and there she was, standing next to Saki's boyfriend. I was like, 'Huh'?"

"So she followed you?" asked Mai. "But why?"

"Unfortunately, we didn't figure this out until later, but it turned out that Saki's idiot boyfriend had threatened her when the rest of us were getting our drinks at the café. He said, 'If you think you can run away, you're dead wrong. You're staying with us until we say you can go, or you'll be sorry.'

"It was really dumb of him, because she must have thought he was threatening to kill her if she tried to leave. And none of the rest of us heard him, so we never thought to tell her that she could go home. We didn't know she thought she *had* to stay with us."

Saki piped up, "But Takaya wasn't serious!"

Yuki silenced her with a glare. "I know that. You know that. But how was Sawako supposed to know?"

Mai took all this in, and then worked up the nerve to ask, "So you didn't tell her to get lost?"

Yuki shrugged. "She seemed to be following us around on her own, and she paid her own way. She wasn't bothering us, so we ignored her. The trouble was, we'd told our parents we were going to stay at each other's houses for the weekend, but we actually went to a resort at Hakone and got hotel rooms. And when we got on the train, Sawako got on too. By the time she arrived at Hakone with us, I figured Saki had befriended her and Saki figured *I* had, so it didn't seem that weird that she was hanging out with us."

"So you had no idea that the police were looking for her?"

"No, why would we? We noticed the news about a missing girl, but it never occurred to us that it was her."

Mai remembered the strange way the detectives had spoken about the case . . . *It wasn't exactly the type of kidnapping that the media claimed it was.* Now it all made sense. It hadn't been a kidnapping at all, but a prank gone wrong.

"But what did Sawako do for those four days?" asked Mai.

Yuki shrugged. "Nothing special. She hung out wherever we were and watched what we did."

"That's it? She just watched?"

This time Saki answered. "Maybe she wasn't used to doing the sort of things we did, going to clubs and so forth. She was looking all around like everything was new to her."

Tomoko said, "You're making her sound all innocent. Actually, she was really creepy."

"Creepy?" echoed Mai.

Tomoko addressed Yuki, as if she had to keep up the appearance of snubbing Mai. "You remember, Saki caught Takuya picking his nose, and she said he was 'a super disappointing boyfriend.' All of a sudden Sawako spoke up, and said some weird thing."

"She quoted Nietzsche." Yuki looked up at the ceiling, as if trying to remember. " 'What we do in dreams, we also do when we are awake: we invent and fabricate the person with whom we associate— and immediately forget we have done so.' "

Tomoko's eyes widened, and the gold glitter she had sprinkled on her eyelids sparkled as her skin moved. "That's incredible, Yuki! You have such a good memory!"

Yuki turned to Mai. "It's not actually as weird as it sounds. She was really into Nietzsche—in fact, she was so into him, her nickname at school was 'Nietzsche.' "

"Nietzsche, the existentialist?"

The teachers at Mai's school had a lot of freedom about what they taught. In her last term, her social studies teacher had spent much of the time covering modern philosophy, and Nietzsche had been one of the philosophers they had studied. But all Mai remembered was what she had needed to know to pass the test, which was that he had been a German philosopher in the second half of the nineteenth century, and was associated with terms like "existentialism" and "nihilism." She certainly didn't recall anything about him likely to spark the obsession of a teenage girl.

Saki curled her lip in disgust at Mai's question. "You're not a Nietzsche fan girl too, are you?"

"I learned about him in school, that's all." Mai turned back to Yuki. "That was actually her nickname?"

"Yeah. They say she got it because of something that happened right after school started this year. I didn't see it myself, but everyone was talking about it.

"Her homeroom teacher said, 'Kioi Academy is one of the most prominent prep schools in Japan. We're different from the other private schools. So sometimes I may make you do things you don't want to do, and study things when you don't understand how they'll be useful to you. But no matter how much you might dislike what you're doing, I want you to believe in me and do what I say, because I know what's good for you better than you do.'

"The teachers at Kioi say stuff like that a lot. It's really annoying. Anyway, it's rumored that Sawako stood up and said, 'Familiarity from a superior embitters, because it may not be returned.'

"Everyone was amazed. The teacher asked her who she was quoting. She said, 'Nietzsche,' and sat back down like nothing had happened. And afterward, no matter what the teacher said, she never spoke up in class again. She just sat there silently with this scary, intense look on her face."

"Wow, that *is* amazing." Mai was impressed by Sawako's nerve, although obviously the other students thought she was a freak.

Yuki's friends exchanged significant glances.

Yuki said, "I only heard about that yesterday. But the really sad part is what happened after that. The next day she came to school looking all cheerful, like nothing had happened. But because she'd acted so strangely in class the day before, everyone thought she was some kind of weirdo, and no one would talk to her. And then she got really mad because everyone was giving her the cold shoulder. And it just snowballed from there. Someone started calling her 'Nietzsche,' and then all the freshmen picked it up, and she ended up an outcast."

Saki grimaced. "Yeah, because she's a total nut."

Tomoko nodded.

Akemi said, "If we'd realized what a head-case she was, we'd never have gotten mixed up with her in the first place."

"Yeah, but we didn't know!" said Yuki angrily.

Her shout drew the attention of the other patrons. Although Mai was the only one who wasn't smoking, she was also the only one wearing a school uniform, so she got the brunt of the judgmental glares.

Yuki said, "If I'd known everyone in her class had been treating her like that, I wouldn't have been so mean to her. All I knew about her was that she had taken my cell phone."

"Yuki . . ." began Akemi.

Yuki lowered her head. Her brown hair fell across her face, but Mai could see how sad she looked. "I think all she wanted was to make friends. She called it *'Chain Mail'* and said it was a role-playing game or something, but I think what she wanted was to connect with someone."

"You know about the website," said Mai.

"Yeah, I looked it up from the e-mail Akemi got," said Yuki. "I'm not that good at writing and I'm not much into reading, so I didn't think of trying it myself. I mean, I wouldn't have even gone to the website if I hadn't been so mad about the whole thing. But when I thought about it later, I could understand how she felt.

"When I was in middle school, I was really rowdy in class. I was smart, but I liked to dress kind of wild, so the teachers didn't like me. And that pissed me off, so I used to do my cram school homework in class instead of following the lessons. They didn't like that, either.

"At first my classmates thought it was funny that I was always ignoring the teachers and talking back in class. But the more the teachers yelled at me, the more I resisted, and eventually everyone decided that I was this weird girl with a chip on her shoulder. I ended up all alone.

"When that happens, you start talking to yourself. Not aloud, necessarily, but when you have no one to talk to, you start having these dialogues in your mind. At least, I did. When I saw the *Chain Mail* site, I thought, 'Yeah, I understand.' Even though there were four people working on it, it seemed really similar to how it feels to make up stories for yourself, and talk to the other 'you' when you're all alone."

With that, Yuki fell silent, and looked down into her coffee cup. Her friends were quiet too.

Mai finally said, "What's up with Sawako now?"

Yuki looked up. Her eyes looked enormous under all her black eyeliner. "Are you going to meet her? What do you want with her?"

"I don't know if I'll do that," said Mai hastily. "I just wondered how she was doing."

Yuki didn't speak for a while, but she examined Mai's face as if it would tell her how much she could say. Then she turned away. "She's been coming to school like always, but she's been wearing funny clothes."

"What sort of clothes?" asked Mai.

"Some old public school uniform. We're allowed to wear whatever we want, and some girls like to wear private school uniforms instead of regular clothes. But no one wears a public school uniform."

"Why do you think she's doing that?"

"I don't know. It might be her way of atoning for having caused such a commotion."

Akemi tapped Yuki on the shoulder. "Hey, Yuki." She indicated with her chin a middle-aged man who was bearing down on them. He was wearing a black suit, and Mai guessed that he was the café manager.

Yuki took the cigarette out of her mouth and stubbed it out in an ashtray. "Mai, you better take off."

"What?" Then Mai realized that Yuki was going to take the fall.

"Just go."

Mai didn't have time to thank Yuki. She could hear the café manager scolding the girls as she fled for the door.

"You girls are underage, aren't you? Let me tell you . . ."

It was raining much harder than it had been when Mai had arrived. But she had been in such a hurry to leave that she had left her umbrella in the café stand.

Raindrops fell on her gray uniform, leaving dark spatters. The marks spread and spread, until everything was black.

MAYUMI

SATURDAY, OCTOBER 18, 9:17 AM.

KODAIRA, MAYUMI'S ROOM.

Mayumi sleepily glanced at the alarm clock next to her pillow. *So late! Why didn't the alarm go off?!*

She hurtled out of bed and threw open the curtains. Black clouds hung low in the sky, threatening a downpour, and it was almost as dark as it had been when she'd gone to bed. No wonder she had overslept—the sun hadn't been there to wake her.

Mayumi looked frantically at the calendar to see what exactly it was that she'd missed. There were red circles drawn around the eighteenth and nineteenth. Today was the first day of the All-Japan Junior Finals. The tournament was at nine in Sendai, so the players all had to get there the night before.

Mayumi laughed.

There was no need to be flustered. She'd already quit the team. She didn't have to go to the gym any more, let alone Sendai.

She hadn't been in her pajamas this late in the day for years, so it was no wonder she'd gotten confused. But from now on, she could always sleep in late on weekends. She could sleep until noon, and spend the entire day listening to CDs and watching DVDs.

"Do your best, Sayuri," whispered Mayumi experimentally. But she felt no regret, no guilt, not even any sadness.

She was surprised that the words didn't conjure the surge of emotions she used to feel. But maybe that was natural. Mayumi had found a place where she could be herself, rather than living in someone else's shadow.

She reached for the cell phone on her desk.

DATE AND TIME: OCTOBER 18, 4:44 AM
AUTHOR: YUKARI
CHARACTER: TETSURO TSUNODA

Hello, Detective Murata.

Are you surprised to get an e-mail from me, after all this time?

I'm not going to tell you how I got your address. I'm sure you're bored with playing puzzle-solving games, and I'm no longer interested in proving how clever I am.

I don't mean to sound cocky. It's like the saying, "One no longer loves a secret once one has communicated it."

I was thrilled when I uncovered your e-mail address. But now, as I write to you, my excitement has faded.

I don't care any more how I learned it, nor should you. We've gone past the point where such things matter.

The important thing is that I have been resurrected, as it were. I slipped past the net you cast and have returned to being my old self.

Perhaps you are curious about how I managed to escape the police searches. I didn't do anything special.

It was your own initiative that did you in.

Why in the world did you tell them to focus on the hills of Izu? Did Sawako suggest that? She wasn't even close.

There's something very wrong with Sawako nowadays.

Maybe it's because she came so close, but then fled from the one who loves her most.

But no matter how it happened, you must have noticed that she's not the girl she used to be.

Sawako really does need me.

I'm going to get her back. No matter what, I'll get her back.

I will not allow you to stand in my way.

No matter how many officers you have searching for me, there won't be enough to overcome the strength of my feelings for Sawako.

You see, no matter how good a police officer's training is, he or she is only a worker doing a job. And people work because they must, so that they can live and eat.

But I'm different. I live only for Sawako.

When I drink, it's so that I may live to watch her. When I eat, it's so I may live to be by her side.

Taking Sawako away from me is the same as killing me. It's the same as telling me to die.

That's why I am infinitely more determined to have her than the police are to keep her from me.

You cannot crush my spirit and it is my spirit which is bound to hers.

But you're not an ordinary cop.

I don't know why, but you seem motivated by more than just a paycheck. I can feel that in you.

```
    That's why I want to talk to you. Before I take Sawako
away forever, I'd like to meet you.

    Please come to the address written at the end of this
letter at 5:00 PM. And please come alone.

    If you want to try to catch me, feel free. But don't
forget that I'm watching every move you make. If you make
it impossible for me to have a quiet talk with you, Sawako
and I will depart on a permanent trip.

    If, by some unfortunate chance, you don't get this
message or choose to ignore it, it goes without saying that
Sawako and I will vanish forever, without warning.

    Finally, if you are curious about how I could manage
to abduct Sawako when she's under police surveillance,
just think about it for a while and I'm sure the answer
will come to you. You are a detective, after all, and all
your instincts have been trained to solve the culprit's
riddles.
```

Mayumi was surprised, but less at Yukari's return from her long absence than by the content of the entry.

"I want to talk to you?" Followed by directions to an address in Tokyo? *What is Yukari saying?*

It was a challenge, that much was clear. But was it a challenge from the stalker Tsunoda to Detective Murata? Or a challenge from Yukari to Mayumi?

The post didn't read like pure fiction. It read more like the one Mayumi had written when she had decided to get in touch with Mai via *Chain Mail*.

Mayumi reread the entry.

Was this e-mail directed at her, rather than to her character? But what did Yukari mean by saying that she was watching Mayumi? Could that be true? And why would Yukari be so angry with her?

Mayumi held the phone to her chest and watched the black clouds shift in the sky. Slowly, an answer came to her.

It might have to do with what Mayumi had been writing. Detective Murata had been fruitlessly pursuing Tsunoda lately. Perhaps every time Mayumi wrote that Murata had been unable to find Tsunoda, or that there had been no contact from him, she had been preventing Yukari from returning to the story. Maybe she had wanted to bring Tsunoda back earlier, but felt that she couldn't as long as Sawako was under police surveillance and Murata hadn't found him.

But would that make her angry enough to want to confront me in person?

Mayumi found that hard to believe. All Yukari had to do to make Tsunoda return was to write an entry where he did. And look how effective his return had been! This was a great, scary post. Was it possible that Yukari didn't understand how the long delay had only made her reemergence more powerful?

Mayumi reread the entry again. When she finished, she was more convinced than ever that it was a message to her.

"I guess I have to go, then," murmured Mayumi.

Meeting Yukari would bring the real and fictional worlds together, which wasn't something Mayumi wanted. But misunderstandings could easily blow up into feuds, and that would be the end of *Chain Mail*. Maybe if she showed up, apologized, and told Yukari how great her writing was, that would make her cool off.

With a sigh, Mayumi wrote down the directions.

MAI
STURDAY, OCTOBER 18, 2:47 PM.
SHIBUYA PARK ROAD.

Mai was not pleased when she once more turned the corner and came face-to-face with Winnie the Pooh.

Dammit! I'm back on the park road again.

It was the third time she had passed the Disney Store. Twice could be attributed to getting turned around, but three times meant she was lost.

She paused on the sidewalk and stuck her hand in her pocket. As people hurried past her, she pulled out and unfolded a crumpled piece of paper that bore the names of a disco, a video arcade, and three clubs. All were crossed out, except for the last club—Genst. It was supposedly behind the Seibu Department Store, but Mai had now walked behind it three times without finding the club.

I can't believe I can't find the last one.

One week ago, Sawako had followed Yuki and her friends to the places written on the paper. Now Mai was retracing Sawako's footsteps.

Everything Yuki had told her only made Mai more interested in Sawako. When Yuki had mentioned that Sawako had taken to wearing an old public school uniform, and that she was the only person at Kioi Academy who did so, Mai's heart skipped a beat. She realized that all she had to do to meet Sawako was to go to her school and look for a girl in a public school uniform . . .

But if she met Sawako, *Chain Mail* would no longer be a separate world. But ever since she'd spoken to Yuki, Mai had longed to meet Sawako.

All of the *Chain Mail* girls were probably loners. But that was no reason for *Chain Mail* to be a place where they would meet in sadness. They hadn't been *driven* out of the real world—its flaws and stupidities had made them leave of their own accord. And so they started talking to the selves within themselves, because it seemed like those were the only people worth talking to.

As Mai walked home in the rain after meeting Yuki, she realized that she, Sawako, Yukari, and Mayumi were all the same. Mai had never imagined that there could be other girls who were so similar to her.

But if that was true, and *Chain Mail* had been the link that bound them together, then it wouldn't be a good idea for them to meet. If they did, their special relationship might vanish, and all that would be left were four ordinary girls with an ordinary friendship, trading gossip about classmates and rock stars. *Loners like us shouldn't try to connect like regular people*, thought Mai.

If she wanted to know Sawako, she could do it from afar—the way they knew each other now. Mai could try to feel what Sawako had felt. They didn't need to actually meet.

So Mai went out to Shibuya to visit the places Sawako had gone with Yuki before they had boarded the train. Mai would see what Sawako saw, and so she could connect with her friend without destroying their fictional world.

"Hey, there. Where ya going?"

The voice dragged her away from her reverie. She looked up. Two young men with bleach-blond hair were standing in front of her, grinning and looking her over.

"You looking for something?" asked the wiry one with spiky yellow hair.

The one with shoulder-length, white-blond hair peered at her note. "Oh, Kentos? What a coincidence, we're going there too."

The short-haired guy grinned at his companion's obvious improvisation. "That's right. Why don't we all go together?"

Mai finally realized that they were hitting on her. Normally, she would have known before they'd even opened their mouths and she'd have quickly walked away. But her heart had been with Sawako and she'd lost her usual snappy reactions.

"Uh, I don't think . . ." she began.

"Oh, don't worry about the cover charge. We'll treat," said Long-Hair.

"Uh-oh, it's raining," said Short-Hair. "We'd better get going."

Short-Hair opened his umbrella, and Long-Hair slithered his arm over Mai's shoulders. His breath and fingers smelled like stale cigarette smoke.

Suddenly those two men, whom Mai normally would have seen as just a moving part of the cityscape, became actual people. Their sleazy physical presence yanked her back into reality.

"I'm not going!" shouted Mai and shoved Long-Hair away with both hands.

Like a rock thrown into a river, Mai's outburst caused a hole in the crowded sidewalk as the other pedestrians moved away and stared. Eventually the other people began to move again and the hollow was swallowed up in an instant.

Idiots! Mai thought. *Why is the world full of obnoxious people?*

Still mentally cursing the men, Mai continued walking down the road. The rain began to fall harder. All around her, umbrellas opened like blossoms, hiding everyone's faces. Her anger abated.

This is no good. I can walk down the paths she took, but that won't make me feel what she felt. All this is just making me into a different sort of groupie.

As she once again circled the Seibu Department Store, she thought, *I have to try to figure out what she was thinking, and what* Chain Mail *meant to her. I should know enough about her from her writing and what Yuki told me to be able to do that.*

She stood at the intersection in front of the statue of Hachiko, the faithful dog, and tried to remember everything she knew about Sawako as she waited for the light to change.

"Nietzsche!" she exclaimed aloud.

An old man standing in front of her turned to look at her. She caught a whiff of the pomander in his hair as he tilted his head toward her. Just then, the light turned green, and the melancholy "walk" tune began to play.* But instead of going forward, Mai turned around and went into the bookshop on Central Street.

"Welcome!" called the young clerk.

"Excuse me," said Mai. "Do you have any books on or about Nietzsche?"

The man's eyes opened wide with surprise, then he pursed his lips and thought about it. "This branch is for magazines and novels, so they're probably not here. If you go to the main store on the other side of Seibu, then . . ."

Another voice interrupted him. "No, some of his books are here. There's a collection way in the back on the second floor."

Mai peered past the store clerk. A small man with white hair stood behind him. The old man was reading at a magazine rack, and had only turned his head to speak. The magazine he was reading was open to a picture of a girl in a sailor uniform. She was lifting her skirt to expose her panties.

The old man added, "Young miss, I admire you for wanting to read Nietzsche at such a young age." His lecherous gaze lingered over her as if she was the girl in his magazine. His skin was covered with wrinkles, like the crackle-glazed vases in her father's pottery collection.

Nasty old pervert! Mai hurried to the second floor, indignant that she'd been helped by a skanky old man with a schoolgirl fetish. For all she knew, he'd made up the thing about Nietzsche so he could watch her ass as she walked away from him.

But he hadn't lied. A set of Nietzsche's books was exactly where he'd said it would be—back wall, second floor. Mai had no idea that Nietzsche had written so many books, and she had no idea where to start. *Thus Spoke Zarathustra, Ecce Homo, On the Genealogy of Morals, The Will to Power*... The titles went on and on.

Wow. They all look intimidating, not to mention expensive, she thought.

One book combined *On the Genealogy of Morals* and *Beyond Good and Evil*. It seemed as good a place to start as any. Her hand could barely close around the thick book. Holding it between her finger and thumb, she headed back down.

The old pervert now stood at the base of the stairs, peering up Mai's pleated skirt. "They were right where I said they'd be, right, little miss?"

He didn't move aside for her to pass. He'd undoubtedly get off on it if she touched him, so she twisted to the side and slipped past as quickly as she could.

It was raining again when she left the bookshop. Even though it was only a little past four, it had gotten very dark outside. The neon signs had gone up early, and the square was lit with videos and flashing neon signs. There were so many people waiting at the intersection that they spilled out into the street. Above their heads, V6 sang their new song on a gigantic screen plastered to the side of a building. On the street corner, a cart lined with bare light bulbs advertised "legal drugs." The young male vendor was talking to thee high school girls, and all of them were laughing so hard that the cart shook.

It was all so tacky and sordid and noisy. *I hate this city and every pervert, drug addict, and hypocritical adult in it!* Mai thought furiously.

She felt like covering her ears and screaming, but instead she reached for her cell phone. As she flipped it open, she automatically hit the "Internet connect" button.

It was kind of ironic—she'd been so obsessed with connecting with Sawako, that it was the first time she'd gotten around to checking the *Chain Mail* site all day.

Mai tapped her foot against the sidewalk as she watched the connection progress bar lengthen. It was so slow! It occurred to her that the definition of a drug addict was a person who couldn't bear to be kept away from drugs. If they ran out, even if it had just been for a few minutes, they wouldn't be able to think of anything but getting more. She wondered if this was what drug addicts felt like as they waited for their next fix.

Is Chain Mail *my legal drug?* Mai wondered. The thought depressed her. *No, it's not like that.* Chain Mail *is my . . .*

The site popped up on her screen, interrupting her thought. There was one new message from Yukari.

The light changed, and everyone crossed the street except for Mai. She stood on the sidewalk, left behind like a forgotten parcel.

MAYUMI

SATURDAY, OCTOBER 18, 4:17 PM.

THE YAMANOTE LINE.

Despite the rain, the train was crowded and noisy with chattering teenagers and adults happy to have the day off. There were a lot of other junior high school students, but mostly they traveled in groups, unlike Mayumi. Most of them were probably headed for the pubs and clubs of Shinjuku, the cosplaying square and trendy used clothing shops of Harajuku, or even Mayumi's destination of Shibuya.

The only person on the train who didn't seem to be prowling for a good time was a girl in a plain, navy blue public school uniform. She was reading a reference book and looked depressed. Mayumi wondered if she was going home after a mock examination. If so, she didn't look like she'd done well.

One group of girls had matching gym jerseys like the ones Mayumi had once worn to complement Sayuri's. Right now Sayuri was participating in a national tournament—the only junior high freshman who'd made the cut. Mayumi wondered how that was going.

"Do your best, Sayuri," she murmured again and smiled.

"We are now approaching Shinjuku," announced the conductor. "Next stop, Shinjuku. You can change trains here to the Chuo, Sobu, and Saikyo lines."

Only four more stops to Shibuya.

Mayumi wondered if anyone had read the *Chain Mail* entry she'd just sent. She had started writing it while she was riding the Seibu line, and had finished it right after she'd changed to the Yamanote line at Takadanobaba station. But the signal on the Yamanote line had been bad, so it took her several tries to send it. She finally managed to post it just as the train pulled out of the Shin-Okubo station.

Mayumi wondered if Yukari would have a chance to read it before they met. But it didn't matter. Either way, Mayumi knew exactly how she wanted the encounter to go.

DATE AND TIME: OCTOBER 18, 4:15 PM
AUTHOR: MAYUMI
CHARACTER: DETECTIVE MURATA

I accept your challenge.

I have no intention of letting you kidnap Sawako, and so you have left me no choice but to confront you.

I will come by myself. I won't call for back-up, and I won't ask for help. I promise you this on my honor as an officer of the law.

Regarding your question about how I would expect you to kidnap Sawako while she's under constant guard, I am not going to attempt to answer it. It's irrelevant, because you will never have the chance to try.

You will never go anywhere with Sawako. I am going to arrest you when we meet today, and then you can sit in jail for the rest of your sorry life and pose your riddles to yourself.

I will see you at 5:00 PM.

Mayumi wondered if her response to Yukari had been too hostile. Yukari did seem to be angry at Mayumi, presumably because Mayumi had made it difficult for Tsunoda to return, so maybe Mayumi shouldn't have stoked the tension between them with her latest entry.

On the other hand, Mayumi's post did continue to drive the story forward. The way it was logically headed, *Chain Mail* would soon reach a climax, and then conclude. Regardless of whether Detective Murata arrested Tsunoda or Tsunoda kidnapped Sawako and hid her away forever, the story would soon be over.

Which was what Mayumi wanted.

It wasn't that she'd gotten bored with *Chain Mail*. On the contrary, it had been a revelation for Mayumi that she could collaborate on story as thrilling as the ones she loved to read. These few weeks of writing had turned out to be far more challenging and fulfilling than six years of badminton.

So she had decided to start it over from scratch. This time she would create the characters and story herself, and then look for other people who wanted to participate. She didn't mind if Sawako and Mai wanted to do it with her again, but she had no intention of alerting Yukari to her new story. Yukari had broken the rules of her own fictional world, and Mayumi wasn't going to let Yukari ruin hers, too.

Yukari was the weak link in the chain, and she had to be cut out.

Mayumi had made that decision when she'd read Yukari's entry that morning. The thought of it annoyed her all over again.

Maybe I should have been even harsher with her, Mayumi thought.

But the thought of a new story, all her own, cheered her up. And since feeling cheerful put her in the mood to write, she decided to work on another entry. She looked down at her cell phone, but she'd lost her net connection. The signal must have gone out when the train had pulled into Shinjuku.

She hit "refresh," and watched the page slowly reload as the train left Shinjuku and headed for Yoyogi. Mayumi was about to go to the "new entry" screen when she noticed that the page had changed. She drew in a startled breath.

```
DATE AND TIME: OCTOBER 18, 4:19 PM
AUTHOR: YUKARI
CHARACTER: TETSURO TSUNODA
    I knew that you would agree.
    This fight is just between the two of us. So let's meet
alone at the appointed place forty minutes from now.
    Please do not do anything to arouse suspicion. I've been
watching you this entire time, after all.
    I'm watching you now.
```

It had only been four minutes since Mayumi had posted her last entry. Yukari must have been holding her cell phone in her hand and hitting "refresh" every thirty seconds to have been able to read it and write a response so quickly.

Without meaning to, Mayumi glanced around the train. A lot of passengers had gotten off at Shinjuku station, but even more had gotten on, so it was quite crowded. Lots of people were looking at cell phones: an old woman with a department store bag, a yawning businessman, a teenage boy, a girl in a navy blue public school uniform, and probably more people who Mayumi couldn't see.

`I'm watching you now.`

Unnerved, Mayumi snapped her cell phone closed. She squeezed her eyes shut and held on tight to the hand strap, letting her body shift with the movement of the train.

Two more stops until Shibuya.

MAI

SATURDAY, OCTOBER 18, 4:23 PM.

THE STARBUCKS AT THE HACHIKO DOG STATUE, SHIBUYA.

Mai's eyes opened wide as she finished reading Yukari's post. *This is turning into a fight*, she thought.

She had been surprised by the confrontational tone of Yukari's original challenge, but Mayumi's response, and then Yukari's fast reply, had each escalated the hostility even further. The characters were speaking to each other directly—or was it Mayumi and Yukari who had gotten into a personal feud?

Mai was pretty sure of the cause. Mayumi and Sawako had been posting frequently in the last week, but in a way that didn't leave Yukari or Mai much room to participate. *Chain Mail* had turned into a story that focused exclusively on Sawako's trauma, Detective Murata's attempts to catch the stalker, and the relationship between the schoolgirl and the cop. All Mai had been able to do was write an occasional entry where Kouhei telephoned one or the other, but she felt as if she was just wedging her character into the cracks of someone else's story. And with Sawako and Mayumi constantly mentioning that there had been no contact from Tsunoda, Yukari must have felt as if her character had been written out entirely.

But that doesn't justify Yukari getting mad enough to challenge Mayumi to some kind of duel, thought Mai.

Nor did Mayumi need to write such a hostile response, when she could have tried to smooth over the quarrel by letting Yukari back into the story.

Mai wondered if the girls were really going to meet. The address Yukari had posted was a video arcade near the top of Spain Hill. It was about a five minute walk away from the Starbucks Mai was sitting in now.

She looked at her cell phone. It was four twenty-three—about forty minutes until the meeting.

But she couldn't decide whether or not she wanted to go. If she showed up, then three of the four *Chain Mail* girls would meet face-to-face. Two of them were looking for a fight, so Mai would have to try to be the peacekeeper—which would undoubtedly make both of them turn their anger on her. And it wouldn't be an exciting, dramatic *Chain Mail* showdown, but a sordid, depressing, real-world squabble.

If Sawako knew what Mayumi and Yukari were doing, she would be so disappointed.

Mai decided to take a crack at the Nietzsche book while she waited. She opened it to the first page. The print was tiny and intimidating, but she held it close to her face and began to read. She didn't understand the first line, but she kept going. She didn't understand the next five lines either.

She could read the text, which was in Japanese, but the content was hard to follow. She plowed on through, but all she could get was that Nietzsche seemed to disapprove of a lot of things. Everything was a "must not" or something like that. "You must not get caught up," or "You must not obsess," or "You mustn't let your heart get stolen away."

But Mai was determined to read at least enough to understand what Sawako saw in the philosopher. She went on reading, pausing to analyze each sentence, and the concentration that it required drove away her worries about Mayumi and Yukari. Still, she didn't make much headway with Nietzsche.

It was stupid of me to buy this book without trying to read a bit of it first. I'm broke now because I spent twelve hundred yen on a book that might as well be in Latin for all I can understand of it.

The other Mai, the Cool Mai in her mind, agreed. *You felt like some kind of detective, trying to feel what Sawako felt. But don't you realize that you're doing exactly what you claim you don't want to do— connect with her in real life? Make up your mind!*

Cool Mai had a point. In a fit of frustration, Mai opened the book to a random page and began reading. It couldn't make any less sense than going in order.

"Both the danger to his life and its reversion to safety were hidden from their eyes. Like this . . ."

Mai took a long sip of her house blend and reread the line. It wasn't that she had suddenly understood it in a flash of intuition; it was that it sounded oddly familiar. She murmured the next line aloud, "A frightening experience brings forth the question of what the people who have experienced the fear *should* be afraid of."

The young woman sitting next to Mai glanced up at her. Mai snapped her mouth closed, then smiled and took another drink to cover her confusion. A light inside her head had decidedly clicked on, illuminating things she had never before been able to see.

She reread the passage, then reached for her cell phone. She connected to the net and logged on to the *Chain Mail* site.

Come on . . . Mai mentally urged the slow connection. *Come on!*

The status bar inched forward, then finally reached its zenith and vanished. The complete set of *Chain Mail* entries came up, with the most recent appearing first. Mai scrolled down the page until she found the part she was looking for.

Finally I told my father. At first he listened carefully and really seemed concerned for me. But then he gave me a talk about how all girls start to feel self-conscious when they become teenagers, and that I had to remember that the only person remotely interested in me was me.

I said it wasn't like that and that I really believed that someone was watching me.

Then he got a funny look on his face—half-worried and half-disgusted—and told me that I must be overly tired and to go on to bed.

Just so you know, when you talk about scary things, people start to think that *you're* the one who's scary.

"That's it!" exclaimed Mai.

The lady next to her stood up. Careful not to look at Mai, she took her coffee to another seat. But Mai didn't care.

That last sentence seemed inspired by the Nietzsche quote Mai had just read. Mai wasn't sure what the significance of that was, but at last she'd found a trail she could follow. She began skimming the Nietzsche book. She still didn't really understand it, but that no longer bothered her.

She was just looking for expressions and lines that she recognized from *Chain Mail*. And once she knew what she was searching for, phrases started jumping out at her, one after another.

Nietzsche wrote, "What we do in dreams we also do when we are awake: we invent and fabricate the person with whom we associate— and immediately forget we have done so."

A girl your age is full of dreams and you can't tell the difference between fantasy and reality. You get an idea of what a person's like, and then you put that image on a pedestal and relate to it instead of to the real person.

Nietzsche said, "The power of instinct is such that when the house is burning, people forget even their noonday meal. But later they haul it out of the ashes."

If God had created us, why had he saddled us with emotions and instincts? Was it to make us suffer? A person whose house has burned down will sit down in the ashes and cry. But a few hours later, he'll sit again in those same ashes and eat. And when he realizes what he's doing, it'll make him so sad that he'll cry again.

In ten minutes, Mai had found three instances where Sawako had paraphrased Nietzsche's ideas. Just like Yuki had said, Sawako really did read Nietzsche, and she understood him, too.

Mai's curiosity about Sawako had grown into a deep respect. And her sympathy for Sawako increased; Sawako, who had been so desperate to find friends, had resorted to stealing another girl's e-mail addresses and sending out a hundred invitations, not knowing who would reply.

No one seemed to have understood her or even liked her. Apparently they'd all thought she was creepy and strange. But beneath the surface of her silence and stoicism, she'd kept believing that somewhere out there were other girls like her.

Mai looked out the windows at the brightly-colored umbrellas and the people hurrying through the intersection in the rain. So many people, none of them paying attention to each other.

"I'm right here," she whispered.

With that, the tension drained out of her.

This is good. This is enough, Mai thought.

This is all I need to know about Sawako's reality. I'm not going to pry into her life any more. If she wanted me to do that, she would have e-mailed me directly. From now on, I'll just connect with her through our fictional world. I'm sure that's what she'd prefer.

I won't go to the video arcade. And if it's not too late, I should e-mail Mayumi and tell her not to go either. That, and to stop writing her part of the story so that it cuts other people out. Because we're not alone in this: we're all connected very strongly now.

Her coffee had gotten cold, but she finished the last swallow as she pulled up Mayumi's e-mail address.

Mayumi, about Yukari . . .

Mai's fingers hovered over the keypad. Since she was going to the trouble of writing, she wanted it to be well written and convincing. Sawako had paraphrased bits of Nietzsche to such good effect in *Chain Mail* that Mai wondered if she should do the same. Surely Nietzsche had some pithy quote she could borrow, on the value of friendship or the foolishness of unnecessary quarrels.

She opened the book again and began scanning the pages. The style was as impenetrable as ever, and it once more impressed her that Sawako not only read it voluntarily, but actually enjoyed it. And as she was musing about how smart Sawako was, Mai's gaze caught something familiar and she stopped.

"The judgment 'good' did not move here from those to whom 'goodness' was shown! It is much more the case that the 'good people' themselves, that is, the noble, powerful, higher-ranking and higher-thinking people felt and set themselves and their actions up as good."

Mai's hands felt cold as she traced her finger down the paragraph. There was something strange about it, but she wasn't sure what made her feel so uneasy. If it was familiar to her, it must be because Sawako had paraphrased it somewhere in *Chain Mail* . . .

She accessed *Chain Mail* and began looking for a similar quote. Before long, she found it . . .

```
That's because right and wrong aren't determined by
personal happiness. It isn't the person who has the good
deed done to them that determines whether it's good or not,
but the person who acts upon them.
```

It was clearly a restatement of the Nietzsche quote. But it wasn't written by Sawako. It was written by Yukari.

What in the world . . . ?

Mai began rereading Yukari's entries. As she did, she noticed that there were times when the stalker Tsunoda waxed philosophical in a way that was very reminiscent of the times when Sawako Shinoda did the same.

```
That bitch. I won't forget about this.
  No, I shouldn't hate her. If I hate her, that's putting
her on the same level as me-maybe even higher. We hate
people who are more powerful than us. So, I despise her. I
hold her in contempt. But I don't hate her.
```

The bit about hating people who are more powerful seemed an unlikely sentiment for a thirteen-year-old girl to come up with on her own, but it sounded a lot like something Nietzsche might write.

Mai riffled through the pages of the book. *Got it!*

"A man does not hate so long as he rates something low, but only when he rates something equal or higher."

There was no denying it. Both Sawako and Yukari had used concepts directly from Nietzsche in their writing. *But what does that mean?*

Mai looked at the busy intersection below her. It was almost five o'clock now, and the streets were so full of people milling about that she couldn't see the asphalt beneath their feet. They looked like ants swarming over a piece of fallen candy.

As she watched the pedestrians maneuvering, Yuki Kanai's words came back to her: "At school, they nicknamed her 'Nietzsche.'"

The crosswalk signal flashed "Don't Walk." Everyone began to hurry. Like drops of water puffing into steam on a frying pan, the people began to disappear, and the asphalt was momentarily exposed. Then cars began to pass along the street and covered the ground with moving metal.

It can't be, thought Mai. *There's no way. It must be a coincidence.*

But she was certain of her conclusion, though it made her body tremble and her breath come harsh and fast. The sounds of her own heartbeats throbbed in her ears, and her skin prickled all over. As she stared out the window, Shibuya wavered before her eyes.

V.

"Assuming a different character can, depending on the situation, be a wise course of action."

MACHIAVELLI
POLITICAL DISCOURSE

Mayumi had arrived at Shibuya station fifteen minutes ago.

It was the first time she'd ever gotten off the train at Shibuya. Yukari's directions had said to leave at the Hachiko exit, but the station was so big that she'd a hard time finding it. When she stopped on the platform to look at the signs, someone bumped into her from behind. When she turned to look, she saw a boy with scarlet-dyed hair and a pierced lip. Instead of apologizing, he clicked his tongue-piercing against his lip-piercing and glared at her. She was too unnerved to say anything. As she watched him walk away, someone else collided with her.

When she finally made her way out of the station, she was immediately accosted by a suntanned young man. "Hey there, where are you going?"

She pretended she hadn't seen him and kept walking. But then another one stepped in front of her. "I've got a great part-time job for you," he offered. "It's not dangerous, and the pay is wonderful."

Unlike most of the teenagers around her, with their dyed hair and piercings and outrageous outfits, Mayumi's hair was natural black, and she wore a pink shirt and un-ripped blue jeans. She realized that everyone could tell from one look at her that she wasn't used to the Shibuya scene, and that made her an easy target for everyone looking to sell something, recruit her for something, or pick her up. She had a hard time just walking away, so she kept getting stuck while people finished their spiel. And then she'd be so nervous, her refusal would come out in a whisper. With all those obstacles, it was five minutes after the appointed time when she finally made it to the video arcade, Game Paradise.

I wonder if Yukari's already here.

Mayumi had hoped to check the place out from the outside. But because it was in a popular area and next to a movie theater, there was no place to stand on the narrow, crowded sidewalk.

Since she had no choice, she stepped inside. Though the area outside was bustling with activity, there were only a few people in the arcade. But it was noisy despite the absence of customers—rap music boomed from ceiling speakers and the video games beeped and buzzed.

Since Spain Hill was especially popular with teenage girls, a lot of the games in the arcade catered to them. A fortune-telling machine and a UFO catcher machine were in the prime spots next to the entrance. The stuffed dolls were piled high inside the UFO catcher, flattening each other out. A row of photo booths made up an entire aisle farther back.

Mayumi looked around for another teenage girl. At first she didn't see anyone. Then she spotted a photo booth with a pink vinyl curtain with a sign saying that it did full-body shots. A small pair of red sneakers peaked out just below the curtain.

Yukari, thought Mayumi. Her stomach tightened.

She had told herself as she rode the train that this meeting was no big deal. But when she saw those shoes and wondered if Yukari was wearing them, it all felt overwhelming. The heavy bass line of the rap song seemed to beat out the panicked rhythm of her heartbeat.

What do I do now? she wondered. *Maybe I should just go home.*

But she was so tense that she couldn't make herself move, either forward to face Yukari or backward to flee. As she stood there and tried to make up her mind, someone suddenly tapped her on the shoulder. Mayumi jumped.

"Mayumi Hattori?"

She turned around. The girl standing behind her had her hair cut in a blunt bob. Her eyes were narrow, her nose was small, and her mouth was drawn tight. For an instant Mayumi thought the girl was Yukari, but then she realized that it was someone she knew.

"Kobayashi?" asked Mayumi.

The narrow eyes became crescent moons as the girl smiled. "Oh, good, you remember me."

Mayumi nodded as she tried to recall the other girl. They had gone to the same elementary school in Kodaira. Kobayashi had been in a different class; she was a gifted student who'd gotten the best grades in the school.

Mayumi had only spoken with her once. Last December, when she had wanted to get into Nihon Joshi Academy, she had asked if Kobayashi would tutor her for the entrance exams. Kobayashi had seemed pleased to help her out. Her mother had recently died after a long illness, so she had been preoccupied and not prone to chit-chat. But she had been an excellent and patient tutor.

But because Mayumi had spent years concentrating on badminton instead of her classes, she was too far behind for a little tutoring to catch her up. After about a week, she thanked Kobayashi for her time and gave up. They hadn't formed enough of a bond during the tutoring sessions to stay in touch with each other and Mayumi had completely forgotten about her.

"How have you been, Hattori?" asked Kobayashi. "It's been such a long time."

Mayumi nodded at her, trying to remember the other girl's first name.

"What are you doing here?"

Mayumi pointed to the photo booths. But when she did so, she saw that the red sneakers had disappeared. Mayumi frantically looked all around the arcade, and finally spotted a girl in red sneakers idling by the UFO machines. If she was making her way out of the arcade, she sure was taking her time.

The girl glanced up, toward the back of the arcade. Her face was pale beneath her shaggy black bangs, and her almond-shaped eyes were as cold as ice. Mayumi was certain the girl was looking straight through her.

"Is something wrong?" Kobayashi inquired.

"What? Oh, no, nothing." Mayumi automatically covered up her distraction, but she had no idea what to do. The girl in the red sneakers must be Yukari, but Mayumi couldn't go over and confront her in front of an old classmate. Also, Yukari had said Mayumi should come alone, but here she was, chatting away with another girl.

Mayumi wanted to go over to Yukari then and there, and explain that the presence of another girl was a total coincidence. But with Yukari already angry, there was no way she'd believe that. From her point of view, this was just another case of Mayumi breaking the rules of the game.

I've got to get rid of Kobayashi, Mayumi thought.

Kobayashi kept talking, apparently not noticing how distracted Mayumi was. "So how do you like Nihon Joshi, Hattori? Do you still play badminton?"

As she spoke, Kobayashi put her hand against Mayumi's back, and gently led her farther into the arcade and away from the girl in red sneakers. Mayumi had no idea how to stop her.

"Badminton? Oh, I quit."

Kobayashi's eyes went wide. "You quit? Why, after all the hard work you put into it?"

Mayumi couldn't even begin to explain when most of her attention was focused on the girl in red sneakers. The girl still stood at the entrance to the arcade, neither making a move to leave nor to play any of the games. She twirled her bangs in her fingers and watched people come and go. It was obvious that she was waiting for someone.

"Hey . . ." Kobayashi gave Mayumi a searching look. "Will you come to the bathroom with me?"

Before she could think of a reason to decline, Kobayashi had steered her into the center of the arcade, toward a bathroom behind the photo booths.

"But . . ." If Mayumi went into the bathroom, she could miss her meeting with Yukari. But what could she say to put off Kobayashi, when the girl seemed determined to have a long-time-no-see intimate session with her?

Kobayashi pushed firmly on her back. "These bathrooms are kind of scary . . . Come on, Hattori, please?"

Mayumi took one last glance at the girl with red sneakers before Kobayashi hauled her into the bathroom. The girl was looking back in Mayumi's direction, and Mayumi thought she looked betrayed as if she was thinking, *You broke your word. I might have expected that from you.*

That's not it! Mayumi wanted to shout. *I'll come back, I promise.*

Then the bathroom door swung closed behind them. There was no one else inside. It smelled like pine freshener. The tiles were wet, as if they had been mopped recently.

Kobayashi leaned against the frosted glass of the door. Her narrow eyes glittered with some suppressed emotion. "So why did you quit badminton?"

Mayumi was overwhelmed by the intensity of Kobayashi's gaze. She opened her mouth and the truth came out automatically. "Well, I was never that good to begin with and I found something else that I liked better."

Kobayashi's thin cheeks twitched. "What's better than badminton?"

Mayumi was frustrated with the whole situation. Back in elementary school, Kobayashi would barely even respond to people when they greeted her, so why was she so intent on having a conversation now? Mayumi wished she'd hurry up and get to the point, if she had one.

I know what to do, Mayumi thought. *As soon as she goes into a stall, I'll go back to the arcade and talk to Yukari. I'll explain to her that Kobayashi is someone I ran into who I used to know in elementary school, and I'll ask Yukari to please wait a little while until I can ditch her.*

Kobayashi spoke so loudly, her voice echoed around the empty room. "I said, what is it that you like better than badminton?"

Once again, Mayumi spoke before she was able to think of a lie. "It's something called *Chain Mail.* You know how you can get online with your cell phone? Well, it's a message board I accessed where me and three other girls are writing a story together. It's kind of like a role-playing game, and kind of like a novel we're co-writing." Mayumi heard her own voice getting higher and faster as Kobayashi just stood there nodding silently. *I have got to stop babbling,* she thought in disgust. "Anyway, that's what it is. Doesn't it sound interesting?"

"Yeah, it sounds like a lot of fun." But Kobayashi didn't sound like she was having any fun as she spoke.

Mayumi gestured at a stall. "Didn't you say you had to go?"

Kobayashi didn't answer. Except for the faint sound of rap music coming from the other side of the door, the girls were enveloped in silence.

"Kobayashi?"

"It might be fun for you, but it's not fun for me." Kobayashi's voice was thick as if she was forcing the words out. She ran her hand through her bangs and pressed her lips so tightly together that they turned purple. "It's not fun having your character stolen away from you, you realize."

"What?" Mayumi had no idea what Kobayashi was so upset about. "What do you mean?"

As Kobayashi stood glaring at her with bloodshot eyes, Mayumi suddenly understood. And in that instant, she remembered. Her old tutor's name was *Sawako* Kobayashi.

Mayumi felt the blood drain from her face. "It can't be . . . You're Sawako from *Chain Mail?*"

Sawako put out both her hands, palms out, and shoved Mayumi hard. Mayumi was taken by surprise and stumbled backward. Her back struck the wall hard enough to take her breath away. She gasped like a fish out of water.

Sawako's stiff, pale face stared down at her. "More fun than badminton?" Sawako spat out. "Of course it was. You stole my character so you could write two parts all by yourself, and run the story exactly the way that you wanted. I bet you felt like the queen of your own little world, didn't you?"

"But you dropped out," Mayumi protested. "I waited for four days, but you never came back. *Someone* had to be Sawako Shinoda."

"I'm Sawako Shinoda," Sawako retorted. "And I *did* come back. But you'd already taken my place."

Mayumi trembled as Sawako edged up closer to her. It was absurd of her to be so frightened—Sawako was just another schoolgirl . . . *Oh no.*

For the first time, Mayumi noticed that Sawako was wearing a navy blue school uniform. A plain old public school uniform, the kind where the skirt only has a few pleats. Three days ago, a girl with that same uniform had stood next to her while she rode the Seibu Shinjuku line.

Today, a girl with that same uniform had been reading across from her while she took the Yamanote line to Shibuya.

I am watching you now.

Those were the lines of Tsunoda, the stalker. But Yukari, not Sawako, wrote Tsunoda.

Then Mayumi understood. "You wrote Yukari's part too?"

Sawako's eyes squinted with fury. Mayumi realized that she was angry on behalf of both herself and Yukari. She was Yukari *and* Sawako too.

Sawako reached into the pocket of her uniform. When she took her hand out, she was holding a small, sharp paring knife.

Mayumi opened her mouth to scream, but fear made her choke up. She tried to step back, but Sawako had her cornered.

Sawako's hand swung out. The blade glittered under the bright white lights.

Japan Times
Sunday, October 19

A thirteen-year-old junior high school girl attacked another thirteen-year-old junior high school girl with a paring knife with a ten centimeter blade, in a video arcade in Udogawa, Shibuya. The incident occurred on Monday, October 18, shortly after 5:00 PM, police officials said. The victim sustained a minor injury to her right arm. The perpetrator was captured by a Shibuya police officer who was patrolling the neighborhood.

The perpetrator is in custody, and is undergoing questioning by the Shibuya police. The police report states that the perpetrator appeared to be disturbed, and was unable to make a coherent statement about the incident. The relationship between the two girls is currently unknown, but some reports suggest that they had argued over an online message board. Further reports indicate that the perpetrator was the victim of last week's missing girl case. The police are taking that into account as a possible motive.

Japan Today
Sunday, October 19

Another violent incident involving minors occurred in Shibuya in a video arcade on Monday, October 18. The arcade is located in a popular section of the downtown area known as Spain Hill. The area is full of boutiques, crepe stands, a movie theater, and other businesses geared toward attracting a teenage crowd. Their efforts are successful, to judge by the numbers of young people who congregate there.

This latest episode involved two teenage girls, one of whom cut another with a knife. According to an eyewitness, the perpetrator was a junior high school girl wearing a public school uniform. She entered the arcade and began speaking to another junior high school girl near a photo booth. The two girls went into the bathroom together.

The eyewitness recalled, "Soon after that, I heard a shout come from the bathroom. It was a girl's voice, saying, 'I can't forgive you.' "

A patrol officer from the Shibuya Juvenile Division happened upon the scene at that moment, and the victim was able to escape with minor injuries. But this had a profound effect on the neighborhood, which has seen other instances of teen violence in recent weeks.

One concerned shop owner remarked, "At this rate, people will think we're on the shady side of town."

A university student said, "This sort of thing happens all the time. Last night I saw two high school boys get in a fist fight. That's Shibuya. It's a risky place full of sketchy characters. But that's why everybody comes here—for the thrill."

It appears that Shibuya will not be granted a quiet autumn.

MAI

WEDNESDAY, OCTOBER 22, 4:15 PM.

YOTSUYA, SUBDIVISION 3, MAI'S ROOM.

Mai threw down the newspaper in disgust. Its pages fluttered from her bed to the floor.

"They don't understand," she muttered to herself.

Why don't reporters actually investigate the stories they write about? What Sawako did had nothing to do with Shibuya—that was just where she and Mayumi happened to meet. Every time some junior high kid commits a crime in Shibuya, does it have to be reported like it's proof that Shibuya is the epicenter of teenage violence?

When Mai had realized that Sawako and Yukari were the same person, she had called Detective Shiota. When she explained the situation to him, he'd agreed to meet her at the video arcade. The police were interested in her revelation because Sawako had been the victim in the missing girl case, but they had only planned to watch her encounter with Mayumi and see how it went. No one had dreamed that Sawako might bring a weapon.

That was the truth behind "A patrol officer from the Shibuya Juvenile Division happened upon the scene."

Yesterday, the police had introduced Mai to Sawako Kobayashi's father.

He had wept as he told her his story . . .

Almost a year ago, Sawako's mother had died of a rare blood disorder. She had spent the previous year in and out of hospitals, undergoing harsh treatments that made her limbs swell and her hair fall out. She had gone to Kioi Academy when she was Sawako's age, and Sawako became obsessed with the idea that it would please her mother if she went there as well.

Mister Kobayashi said, "When we learned that her mother was dying, Sawako began to study even more. She was desperate to make her mother's last months happy ones and she thought that getting into Kioi Academy would do that. She was determined to get first place in the mock exams, and she even asked if she could stop going to school so she could spend all her time drilling for the exams.

"I tried to tell her that it was important for her to spend time with her friends too, and that her mother didn't want her to study all day. But when I did, her face would turn red and she'd argue with me. She'd say things like, 'You don't understand, Father. If I get good grades, that'll make Mama happy,' or, 'If I can make her happy enough, maybe she'll recover,' and, 'I'm doing this for her sake. You don't care whether she lives or dies.'

"Finally, she began to hate me. She developed this fantasy that I was mistreating her mother—that I was beating my wife because Sawako's scores weren't good enough, and that the only way to save her mother was to get the top score on the mock exams."

"Oh, no, that can't be . . ." Mai was at a loss for words.

Mister Kobayashi gave her a weak smile. "It's all right. When people collide with events that they can't bear and can't change, sometimes they'll do anything rather than face their own helplessness. It hurts less to blame someone else. But I didn't realize how far into fantasy Sawako had retreated. I knew she was furious with me, but I thought it was all right. I'd rather have her blame me than someone else. And I thought that if hating me eased her pain, even if it was only a little bit, I wouldn't try to stop her."

As Mai listened with deepening sorrow, Sawako's gentle father explained that he hadn't understood what was going on with his daughter. Hoping that Sawako's anger would recede if he wasn't around as much, he threw himself into his research. He was a university professor who specialized in German philosophy. Sawako had read Nietzsche from her father's bookshelf.

But his absence only made her loneliness more intense, and his well-meaning efforts to let her heal in her own way only pushed her further into madness and despair.

He continued, "I thought our house was too full of sad memories, so I moved us to Yokohama. I had hoped that would help her make a fresh start. But she thought I was trying to break her bond with her mother and she ended up hating me even more. I had no idea what was going on in her mind and I didn't try hard enough to find out. I'm afraid I've been a failure as a parent."

Mister Kobayashi had gone into Sawako's room after she had been arrested and searched her desk. Her drawers were crammed with notebooks, all telling different stories. All the stories were written as if two people were writing them together: Sawako . . . and Yukari.

As he spoke, Mai imagined Sawako sitting at her desk, scribbling intently in her notebook. Sitting by herself, always by herself, under a cold fluorescent light, holding tightly to her memories of her mother, and writing away her loneliness as best she could.

"She learned how to use a computer at Kioi Academy," he said. "Her teachers told me later that she hadn't been able to make any friends, so she spent a lot of time in the computer lab. I looked at the *Chain Mail* site last night and I was amazed that she'd created it all by herself."

He shook his head sadly. "She's a very talented writer, don't you think?"

Mai could only nod.

After Mister Kobayashi went home, Detective Shiota had spoken with Mai for a while . . .

"Sawako taught herself how to create a website from a book she bought," Detective Shiota said. "She created the message board and sent herself the first message, under the name 'Yukari.' That's why I think that she originally intended to play all four roles herself."

"I think so too," replied Mai.

Mai was an only child, so she understood what it was like to spend a lot of time by herself. When she had no one to talk to or play with, she would ask herself questions and answer them, or play two or three roles in a story in her mind. She had "Cool Mai," and Sawako had "Yukari." But Sawako took it outside of her mind and created *Chain Mail*.

If Sawako hadn't happened to pick up Yuki Kanai's cell phone, *Chain Mail* probably would have been her own lonely story. There were more than a hundred people listed in Yuki's address book. Not all of them were true friends, but Sawako must have been overwhelmed by the realization that Yuki knew so many people, however slight the connection might have been.

When she imagined how Sawako must have despaired at that moment, Mai felt as if a tight band wound around her heart.

Every day for Sawako must have been so lonely. But even without friends, she had found a way to survive. Sometimes she was Sawako, and sometimes she was Yukari, and as long as they could write their stories together, she could tell herself that everything was fine. But when she saw Yuki's address book, she was no longer able to fool herself.

In that moment, she longed to be connected to people who weren't invented somewhere inside her. It didn't matter if they never met in person, as long as she could talk to someone other than herself. And so she took Yuki's address book and e-mailed everyone in it, asking them if they wanted to create a fictional world.

Mai was sure that Sawako hadn't meant any harm by it. She must have longed to receive an answer, but the only person from Yuki's list who had responded was Mai.

Mayumi hadn't been in Yuki's address book. Detective Shiota told Mai that Mayumi and Sawako had gone to elementary school together, and Mayumi had asked Sawako to tutor her when she was trying to pass a difficult entrance examination to get into Nihon Joshi Academy. But Mayumi had given up on her hope of passing the exam after a week of tutoring. Soon afterward, Sawako moved to Yokohama, and the girls lost touch.

When Detective Shiota had taken Sawako to the juvenile detention facility, she had spoken very little. But when he asked her about her previous relationship with Mayumi, her face lit up. She had spoken of Mayumi as if she was an old friend whom she hadn't seen for a long time. Though Sawako had only hung out with her for a week, she had kept Mayumi's e-mail address.

Detective Shiota rubbed his eyes. "And Sawako wouldn't tell us why she hurt her only friend. Mai, do you know what went wrong between them?"

Mister Kobayashi had asked Mai the same question. "I don't understand. She actually made friends with you and Mayumi, right? It wasn't like her notebooks, where she was only writing to herself. So why would she attack her friend? And her only friend from elementary school, too."

Mai hadn't been able to answer that question at the time, but she figured it out later, after going over all the *Chain Mail* entries. For the four days that she had been with Yuki Kanai and thought she couldn't leave, Sawako hadn't had her cell phone with her, and had been unable to post any new entries to *Chain Mail*. Mayumi, who was so good at imitating the style of American mystery writers, must have assumed that Sawako had given up on the project, and had begun writing under Sawako's name and in her style. When Sawako had returned, she found that her place in *Chain Mail* had been usurped.

Though Mayumi had been Sawako's first real-life friend, the story itself had taken the place of real friends in Sawako's heart. All the stories she'd written had been like friends who helped her deal with the pain of losing her mother, being estranged from her father, and her own bitter loneliness. When Mayumi took over her role in *Chain Mail*, it was as if one friend had stolen away that outlet. Sawako's anger and sense of betrayal must have driven her to attack Mayumi. It was a sad and ironic ending to the story, and not one that Mai would have written.

Though Mai knew that what Sawako did was wrong, she couldn't find any hatred in her heart toward her. Instead, Mai couldn't help but sympathize.

Sawako didn't know how to deal with her own anger. Since she had no friends, she didn't have experience with either quarrels or forgiveness. Without friends, she couldn't know the release of shouting, "I never want to see you again!" Nor could she have known the regret that comes later or the relief of being able to apologize and make up. Since the business of fighting was new to her, she didn't know how to do it in a safe way. So instead of shouting at Mayumi, she had used a knife.

But as much as Mai empathized with Sawako, she didn't think Mayumi had done anything terribly wrong. Detective Shiota had told Mai all about Mayumi's own sad story. It seemed that Mayumi had spent years standing in her best friend's shadow, devoting herself so whole-heartedly to supporting her friend that she'd had no time left for her own interests.

"Mayumi said that she kept telling herself that her best role was as Sayuri's right hand girl, but some small part of her wanted to have her own day in the sun," Detective Shiota explained.

Mai nodded.

"I can understand that," said Detective Shiota earnestly. "Something like that happened with me when I was young. I started studying *kendo** when I was a child, but I was never very good at it. From elementary school to college, I was always the back-up to the back-up. Part of me thought, 'Maybe I should quit and practice something I'd be better at,' but another part of me thought, 'I should keep on trying hard, and who knows? Maybe some day I'll be good enough to compete.' Those two voices fought inside of me for years."

After speaking with both Detective Shiota and Mister Kobayashi, Mai understood everything: the loneliness that led Sawako to create "Yukari" and the bewildered rage that drove her to violence; Mayumi's longing to be the center of attention and use her own talents, which made her take over the main character of *Chain Mail;* and Mai's own alienation from her parents and other teenagers that made her cling so tightly to the new friends she'd made.

Mayumi hadn't realized that the Sawako of *Chain Mail* was the same Sawako who had tutored her in elementary school. The

---

* The Japanese martial art of fencing with bamboo swords.

knowledge that she had been attacked and injured by an old friend came as such a shock to Mayumi that for several days after the incident, she'd been unable to speak. Her wound had healed, but the emotional damage had cut deeper than Sawako's knife. Mayumi still hadn't returned to school.

The newspapers and magazines had reported on the story with easy catch-phrases like, "today's Internet society," and "rampant teenage violence," and "alienated youth," but Mai didn't think any of that garbage came near the truth.

"We were all a little bit strange," she whispered.

Not only Sawako and Mayumi—I am too. My parents let me run wild, but I wish they wouldn't; my club friends chase after singers, but I only want to listen to the music. And there's no one I can talk to who might see things the way I see them.

Mai, Sawako, and Mayumi all had trouble dealing with reality, and had only been able to connect with each other through fantasy.

Was there something wrong with them? Or was the problem with a society that didn't accept them? Or did both sides need to reach out more?

Mai had been reading the newspapers every day, searching for an answer. But all she found were empty words about "shoddy post-war education" and "the dilapidation of the cities' effect on youth." None of them wrote anything that rang true.

In the end, she could find no answers. All she knew was that she had lost some precious friends.

I don't want people to think I'm weird. But I can't pretend that none of this happened. I can't just walk away.

There was no law that said that only face-to-face encounters were meaningful. The reality of newspaper articles and bullying classmates and sports teams wasn't the only reality in existence.

I'm not running away from reality, thought Mai. *But I'm not going to settle for just one.* She knew now that there were other people like her. *If you make your own world, then you can connect with kindred spirits.*

Some day, Sawako might come back. Until then, I wonder if anyone else out there would like to play?

Mai booted up her computer and connected to the Internet. A message board filled up her homepage.

It was a new *Chain Mail* site.

Mai had created it. It had taken her three days of sitting at the computer with a how-to manual open in her lap.

Hi, I'm Mai. I'm a girl in my third year of junior high.

Are there a lot of things that annoy you? The stupid, pretentious media bugs me, but what bothers me the most are some of the teenagers I know and hypocritical parents . . .

Mai scrolled down the page. She didn't expect anyone to have signed up yet. She had only finished creating the site the day before, and last night she'd sent off e-mails telling people about it. She had sent them to everyone in her address book—about a dozen people.

But she couldn't help hoping.

There are four characters the participants can play.

Heroine	( )
Her tutor/boyfriend	(Mai)
The woman detective who pursues the stalker	(Mayumi)
The stalker	(Yuki)

"No way!" exclaimed Mai.

She stared at the screen until her vision became so blurred that she could no longer read the names of her friends. Then she threw her arms around the monitor and allowed her tears to fall.